WRITERS WHO SUCCEEDED THANKS TO FRAN SHAW'S EXCITING NEW METHOD

Bob Z. (buyer) "I did the experiment and wrote a really effective letter. It got me the interview . . . and the job!"

Lynn P. (college student) "You were so right about free-flowing writing. It's wonderful! Especially when those gems come out."

Hank P. (businessman) "My stuff is shorter now. It says what I want it to say and gets the job done better."

Bill P. (art designer) "I really like writing now— and for me that's a great thing."

30 WAYS TO HELP YOU WRITE

by
FRAN WEBER SHAW, Ph.D

BANTAM BOOKS
TORONTO · NEW YORK · LONDON · SYDNEY

30 WAYS TO HELP YOU WRITE
A Bantam Book / November 1980
2nd printing .... October 1981
3rd printing .. September 1983

ISBN 0-553-24073-0

Published simultaneously in the United States and Canada

PRINTED IN THE UNITED STATES OF AMERICA

H   12 11 10 9 8 7 6 5 4 3

To My Family

Contents

ESPECIALLY FOR WRITING CLASSES[1]

	Try Experiments
•a first class to get acquainted	7 (Steps 4, 5)
	8 (Step 1)
•writing "free-flow" together	1, 2, 3, 4
•blackboard group writing	15, 16
•outdoor group poem	5
•finding a subject and getting going	28, 29
•getting into any area for discussion	15 (Version 2)
•library treasure hunt	19, 26
•writing about men and women	20
•writing dialogue	13
•writing description	6, 7, 8
narration	9, 10, 11, 12, 13, 14
exposition	16, 17, 18, 19
argument	20, 21
•writing about literature	25
•writing term papers and reports	24, 26
•writing essay exams	27
•revising	30 (see Part IV)
•writing effective letters (getting someone to do something for you)	22, 23
•writing an essay on an application	28, 29
•get some feedback from others	18, 21, 22, 24
•interview people, then write	17, 20

---

[1] NOTE TO TEACHERS. For a change of pace, begin class with a writing experiment. Have students read aloud part or all of their own or each other's papers. Then ask what the students like about the piece read? What works well?

If you prefer, suggest doing an experiment at home to generate material for essays and stories.

WHAT DO YOU WANT TO WRITE?

	Try Experiments
•the first draft of anything	28, 29
•a paragraph to get going	1, 2, 3, 4
•a letter that gets action	22, 23
•a story	1, 3, 7, 8, 9, 10, 11, 12, 13, 14
•a poem, or a "group poem"	5, 11, 13, 15
•an autobiographical essay	9, 10, 11, 12, 17, 20
•a "how–to" article	18
•a letter to the editor	21, 22, 23
•a speech	16, 28, 29
•a promotional piece	28, 29
•an essay exam	27
•a research paper	19, 28, 29
•a paper for history, social sciences, or humanities	19, 26
•an essay about literature	25
•a scientific or technical report	24
•a memo in plain English	23
•a comparison/contrast	17, 26
•an essay for a college, job, or fellowship application	28, 29
•a description of a place or person	5, 6 7, 8
•a long report or dissertation	24, 28, 29
•an abstract or summary	24
•a clear version of a confusing sentence	30

ACKNOWLEDGMENTS

Thank you so much Barnett Weber, Elizabeth Weber, David Shaw, Joe Cary, Tren Anderson, Lee Jacobus, Peter Elbow, James Jenkins, Joelle Delbourgo, John Owens, and especially Terry Winter Owens. Your encouragement, above all, helped me help myself write.

Preface

When you put words on paper, is it like pulling teeth?

You're not alone. Ask people what happens to them, and you'll hear: "I panic," "I can't get going," "What comes out on the page just isn't as good as what's in my head."

But many of these same people are learning how to help themselves write, how to build confidence, save frustrating hours, and have a better time writing.

Would you like to

—discover a way to write what you want anytime?

—get from first notes to final draft, painlessly?

—experience your creativity now?

These experiments are designed to give you a new ease and skill in writing. Try a few and you'll see you already have a wealth of material which can just pour out. You'll learn how to become your own best friend when you write. Instead of struggling, you can create a new condition from which words freely flow. You'll find the experiments especially useful if you're

—a student with an essay due

—a teacher trying to generate lively writing

—a business person who needs to communicate more effectively

—a housewife with an important letter to send

—an aspiring writer who hopes to get going.

People who've tried these experiments at schools, corporations, and writers' conferences tell me they have a fresh taste of words coming easily—they're delighted with the results.

Dr. Bruce Sherman, for instance, never thought of himself as an author. Last summer, he played with writing "free-flow" at the beach and he enjoyed it so much, he began writing this way in a weekly column. This year he landed a prestigious job which includes producing a newsletter for dentists across the country.

Solomon P., a teacher at the local community college, tried writing "three-liners" with a group from the Neighborhood Youth Corps. At first, it was just a pleasant break from routine. But students quickly joined the experiment, and were proud of the "group poem" they wrote together. They asked, "When can we do another one?"

Tom L., who'd "rather do anything than write," had the chance to publish an article. To inspire himself, he typed out a question he wanted to answer, let tensions "drain" from his body, then "talked" nonstop on paper. "I can't believe it. I wrote more in ten minutes than I had written in my whole life."

Talented undergrad Lynn P. complained she'd been feeling stuck for months. I received a card last Christmas: "You were so right about free-flow writing. It's wonderful. Especially when those gems come out."

Returning to college after 15 years, Helen A. felt lost when she had to do her first paper. She phoned to say, "I tried the experiment for writing a comparison. Instead of wondering, I knew just what to do. I got a 95—and a note from my teacher saying, 'If you haven't thought about writing, you should.'"

Another continuing education student Diane M. told me she never found enough time to do all her work. It took her weeks to gather material for even a short essay, and she usually got sidetracked in the overflow. I showed her how to divide a paper into sections and plan her pages. "It's working! I had a paper due last week. What would've taken me twenty hours, I did in two."

An overdue Ph.D. thesis was depressing Steven R. "You know how long I've been trying to get this done? Seven years." He told me he had "all the data," so I asked him to write nonstop "the section you feel you can do right now." Exhilarated after finishing the whole first draft, he told me, "I consider myself a difficult case— I just didn't want to write it. But once you got me going, it was exciting. It felt good to watch it get done. Now I know I can turn out anything I have to."

Says Jane R., "I wish I'd had this book in college—all that wasted time!"

Bob Z., a buyer for a bookstore chain, wanted a better job. "I did the experiment and wrote a really effective letter. It got me the interview and, I think, the job." After a series of business writing workshop sessions, he told me, "I look at the writing I did six months ago. I edit and organize my thoughts better. The tone I'm putting across is much more effective. I think of who the reader is going to be, and step into his shoes for a moment. And when I read now, I can see where people with good points get lost in their writing. And I know how to help them."

Hank P., who trains people to use medical equipment, agreed. "My stuff is shorter now. It says what I want to say, and gets the job done more quickly."

Art designer Bill P. said he was grateful. "I really like writing more than when I started—and for me that's a great thing."

After a workshop at his company, systems analyst Darryl P., pleased with his brisk new writing style, summed it up with a smile: "This is great."

Whether you're a "non-writer" who must get a job done or an aspiring author who's feeling stuck, you'll find experiments here to suit your needs. Practice the ones that work best for you, and begin to build a new image of yourself: soon you'll know you too can write whatever you want.

Fran Shaw

PART 1

NOTICING MORE AND HAVING PLENTY TO SAY

Every time you sit down to write, you need to experience words coming easily. It feels good to sail across the page, something quickening inside as ideas pour out. And it's just this momentum that keeps you writing.

But how to begin? You've read, thought, made notes, you want to write. Yet you put it off all day. Finally, you sit down and eke out a few sentences . . . and scrap them.

Familiar?

Look at it like this: you may be suffering from acute writing anxiety. That's when you say to yourself "I can't" even before you try. A teacher of mine calls it "teacher-itis." "When you were younger," she explained, "someone said that you were good at one thing but not at another. Good in math, but not in English. And now you tell yourself, 'I can do this, I can't do that.' Maybe it's not so!" The main symptom: believing that voice that jumps in to comment even *before* you begin ("I can't") and especially while you write ("This is no good"). It stops you dead.

What a moment of possibility! Here's a sly way to avoid that, and get going. As an experiment, before writing, turn your attention away from the task for a moment, and *focus on your body and senses now*. Doing this, you'll clear a space, make room for a fresh impulse.

You may notice that those thoughts which have you stuck are mirrored in your physical self. Now as you read, for instance, are you holding your jaw tightly? Keep it like that a moment, then let it relax. Your new approach is as simple as that. You may not be able to talk yourself out of discouraging speculations, but what would happen if you took a few minutes—before writing—to "unlock" muscular tension? Would words flow more freely? While you give your body a few minutes of attention and re-

3

laxation, you're no longer fretting or criticizing. You're not stuck in that. Circulation, muscular tension become different: you create a new condition in yourself.

"Try an experiment? Relax my face? Sounds interesting, but I haven't got time. I better just dig in and do it my old way."

You've heard that voice before. It's the one that makes you tense up. Once again you're about to, ugh, make spinach out of a writing task.

Why not save all those unproductive hours straining? Try an experiment; you'll discover things you didn't know a moment ago.

"Experimenting" means you don't know what will come. You open, in a specific way, to your experience and don't have to figure out what you'll write. In fact, by treating yourself like an undiscovered genius, you may discover your best ideas come when you're "playing" rather than forcing.

For now, don't edit or criticize *while you're writing:* that'll happen later. At the moment, you want only to write abundantly without concerning yourself about impressing some future reader. Give yourself the chance to see how you can use the process of writing to feel more alive and express that intensity.

Whatever you want to write, take ten pleasant minutes now to try a first experiment.

Experiment 1
Write free-flow for the pleasure of now

"Now I'm Sitting Here"

1. Sit comfortably, perhaps outdoors. Write across the top of your pad: "NOW I'M SITTING HERE AND." Put down your pad and pen. Read steps 2, 3, and 4, and try them.

Relax, Head to Toe

2. Close your eyes, and allow the muscles of your face to relax. Move down your body, naming to yourself each part and suggesting it relax. It's as if tensions can drain

4

down and out your feet. (Don't worry about how much you can relax—that's not important.)

3. REALLY LISTEN to sounds from all directions, as if nothing else matters but hearing everything.

4. Very slowly open your eyes. Pick up your pen and start "TALKING" nonstop on the page. When you don't know what to say next, DESCRIBE sounds, smells, tastes, tactile sensations, and sights now. Keep your pen moving for two pages, and stop.

5. Read through, and underline highlights, anything you like, whatever strikes you. (To take it further, use *he* or *she* instead of *I*; or see "Shaping What Comes," p. 9.)

Did you notice
   —*how it is possible for you to cover a page with words?*
   —*how to build momentum?*
   —*where in your writing you sound really sure?*
   —*if more is available to you when you're not harnessed to a task but free to explore any direction?*

Here's a sample by someone who's done a lot of free-flow writing. The writer tried Experiment 1 by a waterfall:

A rush of waters, crash and flow. Watching from a log above the falls. Below, white water coursing in all directions, pushing through rocks for an outlet. I'm noticing the rise and fall of my chest, a fly darting about, the heat of the sun on my arms. The sun is just atop the overhanging foliage—green leaves in

5

motion against blue sky. The foaming river rushes up against a large brown boulder. . . .

She cast it into the third person to see if it suggests a story:

A rush of waters, crash and flow. Jenny watched from a log above the falls. Below, white water coursed in all directions, pushing through rocks for an outlet. Jenny, too, was testing for direction. As she watched the foaming river rush up against a large boulder, she thought of Peter. Could she wear away his resistance?

Try Experiment 1 ten minutes a day for a week, at different hours or in favorite places. Begin an Album of You. Or write this way while music plays. You'll notice each time you do that conditions within you seem different. It's a new current you're feeling and the current is strong!

The more you try, the more you see how to build momentum. You'll write some surprisingly well-turned phrases, and get confident. Producing words this way is like doing scales on a piano when you want to become a pianist.

BUT WHAT ABOUT THOSE 500 WORDS DUE FRIDAY?

If you have an essay, report, proposal, or letter to write, get going by FINDING THE QUESTION you are able to answer. Turn to Experiment 28, p. 122, to discover how to write 500 words about anything.

Where else should you look for material? As you try experiments and begin writing an essay or story, ideas for other things to write may come to you. Don't let them slip by. What someone says may spark a memory, or you'll overhear a bit of conversation—a new subject will probably occur to you. Before going back to what you're working on, jot down a few lines on anything handy; later, put it in an "Ideas" folder. Or you may read something that interests you in a newspaper or magazine: a funny incident, a statistic, a scientific discovery, an unusual item about a person or event or pet subject. Tear out the article and put it in a "Clippings" folder. Don't count on remembering: always record your idea. When you feel like writing, you can look through these folders for stimulation.

Even more stimulating is a vivid, heightened experience now which will give you plenty to say, and get you in motion. Choose one of the next five experiments, and try it step by step.

Experiment 2
Walk "blind" to discover more

---

1. Ask someone to take you on a Blind Walk.[1] Cover your eyes with a scarf. Your guide takes you by the hand.

2. WALK BLINDFOLDED in silence. Let your guide hand you things to touch.

3. After ten minutes, take off your blindfold but keep your eyes closed. SIT down and SENSE the palms of your hands . . . and the fingers. . . .

4. Very slowly OPEN your eyes just a crack at first, then halfway. Eyes open, look at your hands. Freely WRITE your experience from beginning to end.

Did you notice
  —*what you felt when you took your first steps, and how this feeling changed?*
  —*which of your senses seemed to be working more?*
  —*your first thought or visual impression when you opened your eyes?*
  —*anything new about something familiar, as if experiencing it for the first time?*

---

[1] A technique for expanding awareness, suggested in Lewis and Streitfeld's *Growth Games* (New York: Bantam Books, 1970).

Experiment 3
Continuously sense each step

1. STAND for a moment SENSING the contact of your feet and the ground. Sense your big toe, other toes, ball of your foot, arch, heel. (You can try this barefoot if you like, or with one shoe off.)

2. WALK for five minutes trying to be aware, through sensation, of each foot touching the ground (but don't look at your feet). When something distracts you, focus again.

3. STAND for a moment still aware of your feet on the ground. RETURN, knowing each footstep.

4. Sit down, and WRITE across the top of a page: "I was walking." Midway down the page write: "And then it happened."

WRITE NONSTOP completing the first sentence. When you get halfway down the page, let your imagination take over. Keep writing! Stop after two pages.

Did you notice
—how many times you really had a sense of your feet and the ground? what took you away?
—anything unusual about the surface you walked on?
—how walking with a focus helps you experience more?

Experiment 4
Look for one color

1. Take a Yellow Walk or a White Walk. That is, as you walk, look for things of one color.

2. The instant you notice something yellow, it's as if a camera clicks, and you're in the picture. Write down what you see and also something about yourself now (how you're standing, your facial expression, what you're thinking or feeling).

8

3. Walk for ten minutes making notes.

4. Sit down, read what you have, and WRITE NON-STOP. Describe your walk from beginning to end, or perhaps write a poetic catalogue of all these things of one color.

Did you notice
   —if you saw more when trying to look for one color?
   —whether any objects reminded you of another time or place?
   —anything in nature that seemed to "say" something about your life?

SHAPING WHAT COMES

Your free-flow writings may become part of a story or essay, so keep them (as is) in your "writings" notebook. You'll find you'll accumulate a wealth of personal material which is your own natural resource. One woman, for example, "mined" her notebook and arranged seven short pieces as one "crisis" week in her character's life. A businessman was able to use a whimsical bit about the Great Pumpkin as the opening anecdote for a speech. So keep writing for the fun of it—without criticizing what comes—and you'll have something to work with when you need material.

If you'd like to take one of your writings and shape it into a paragraph or short essay, try this:

1. Choose a piece you really like, and read it over.

2. What did you realize from this experience? Sum up your MAIN IMPRESSION in a sentence and say it out loud as if telling a friend.

3. Compare that sentence with the first one already on the page. Which gives your point of view, your slant on this experience? Would a reader want to hear more? Use that to lead off.

If you don't like either, ask an intriguing question.

4. Begin a new paragraph each time you bring in another idea, shift gears, or describe something happening suddenly.

5. Cross out in pencil any details or sentences which don't have anything to do with the main impression you want to convey.

6. End with a sentence you sound sure of. Make your point about what you've discovered. Title this piece, and type it up.

If you'd like to begin a story, try this:

1. Name your main character.

2. Cast your free-flow writing into the third person (use *he* or *she*), and see if it suggests a story. Now it's your main character that's sitting, or walking, or thinking about things, or noticing the surroundings.

3. Try to convey a particular mood by the way your character sees what's around, by what she's thinking. Cross out sentences which don't fit. Add others which might suggest what her problem or situation is at this moment.

4. Write just the first page of your story. Rather than plan what you'll say, let it unfold: just keep writing.

A word about point of view. Your point of view reveals your impression or appraisal of an experience. It's like your particular pair of glasses that tints what you see a certain color. The reader sees the world through your eyes. Also, a point of view can orient your reader in time and space: you view a scene from a specific point on a hillside on a summer morning, for instance, and describe the panorama. Or, your point of view can be your feeling about an experience. For example, walking blindfolded terrified you at first, and each step meant danger.

Or, in a story, the point of view has to do with which character you let witness and tell what happens. Does the young widow tell her own story, in diary form, or is the story told from the point of view of her teenage son?

That is, do you write in the first person (*I*), the second person (*you*), or the third (*he, she, one, it*)? It's most important not to jump around too much. If you choose *I*, don't shift to *you*. Don't write: "*I* never realized how little I notice of the world around me. *You* don't hear or see half of what's happening." If you write, "*He* watched the sunlight play on the leaves," don't add, "*You* could see each vein."

A reminder: when shaping these first writings, be faithful to your experience and to the voice in which you first expressed it. Your own voice has power. A quality of emotion comes through, a rhythm of words, that holds the writing together. For now, keep writing in your natural voice. Later you can try describing the same event from the point of view of other people there. Or you might try on new voices for special effects.

Here's how one professional writer shaped material from a walk. In his story, a boy comes home from school. What main impression comes through—in a word, how does the world look to the boy?

Twigs of bushes leaned over the walls; the little hard green winterbuds of lilac, on gray stems, sheathed and fat; other branches very thin and fine and black and desiccated. Dirty sparrows huddled in the bushes, as dull in color as dead fruit left in leafless trees. A single starling creaked on a weather vane. In the gutter, beside a drain, was a scrap of torn and dirty newspaper, caught in a little delta of filth: the word ECZEMA appeared in large capitals, and below it was a letter from Mrs. Amelia D. Cravath, 2100 Pine Street, Fort Worth, Texas, to the effect that after being a sufferer for years she had been cured by Caley's Ointment. In the little delta, beside the fan-shaped and deeply runneled continent of brown mud, were lost twigs, descended from their parent trees,

11

dead matches, a rusty horse-chestnut burr, a small concentration of sparkling gravel on the lip of the sewer, a fragment of eggshell, a streak of yellow sawdust which had been wet and was now dry and congealed, a brown pebble, and a broken feather. . . .

(from Conrad Aiken's
"Silent Snow, Secret Snow")

PART 2

FREEING MATERIAL FOR DIFFERENT KINDS OF WRITING

You didn't have to pay, it . . . I just finished paying for it."

He started to walk out and as he passed me, he
reached down and touch my shoulder. "Thanks,
Why didn't you pay it

Chapter 1
Describing People, Places, and Things

When you don't know what to write, or can't find the words, consider whether your senses are working at full pressure.

A rich sensory experience yields a wealth of simultaneous impressions which call for words to convey that intensity. A writing experiment can help you discover the route to greater experience so you'll find your way whenever your material seems insufficient.

It's best to start simply. Take your cue, as I do, from the haiku poets who express in only seventeen syllables a powerful moment of experience. It's something like taking a snapshot of what is right now, without being general or abstract, such as Basho's famous haiku which translates:

> The old pond,
> A frog jumps in—
> Plop![1]

Or Gyodai's:

> Snow is melting . . .
> Far in the misted mountains
> a caw-cawing crow.[2]

It's almost as if it's the poet's role to be the eyes and ears by which the universe perceives itself.

By writing short "imagist" or "haiku" poems, you

---

[1] Transl. by R. H. Blyth, *Zen in English Literature* and *Oriental Classics* (N.Y., 1960), p. 217.
[2] Quoted in *Cherry Blossoms* (Mt. Vernon, N.Y., 1960), p. 7.

15

stretch your descriptive abilities, and see how to focus on the startling particular. As with essay writing, it helps to warm up by doing a page of free-flow writing (Exp. 1, p. 4). Perhaps the most useful thing you can do is first "clear a space" by creating a new condition in yourself.

A preliminary relaxing exercise will give you a fresh start. You'll feel tensions and thoughts draining out of your body, and your senses opening more. As the first step of any writing experiment, take five minutes for yourself and allow a wave of relaxation to flow over you. Practice this so you can do it any time.

OPENING EXERCISE

Sit comfortably, and close your eyes.
Allow the muscles of your face to RELAX.
    Move slowly down your body, silently
    relaxing each part from HEAD to TOE.
LISTEN a while to sound coming in from
    all directions, as if nothing else matters
    but doing that.
Slowly open your eyes, and do the next ex-
    periment.

Experiment 5
Write "three-liners" to notice what's here

You can try this experiment by yourself or with others.

1. Go to a favorite place outdoors. Open with your relaxing exercise (above).

2. Without turning your head, notice what's in your peripheral vision along with what's in front of you.

3. Write phrases, one on each line, in groups of three lines, that convey vivid details of this place now.

Try this with others to create a "group" poem:

16

4. Choose your best three tiny poems and number them one, two, three.

5. Move into a circle. Have each person read aloud her number one, going around the circle. Go around again, reading number 2, and then around once more, reading number 3.

Did you notice
—if you captured the flavor of the season?
—which "tiny poems" seem like snapshots?
—how many of your senses came into your writing?
—a sequence in what you wrote? would you re-arrange?

Here's part of a group sequence written one summer morning at the beach.

from BEACHWRITING

Hot sand,
   a radio blaring;
      a wave rolls in and breaks.

         Distant children's voices,
            tide riding over sand flats,
           hazy horizon.

Green moss on brown rock,
   two gulls flapping silently by,
      sunlight glints on little waves.

         Wet hair,
           salty tongue;
            life guards watching.

Seaweed perfume,
   snails and crabs creep;
      waves waving!

Blue and white water,
glistening minerals,
broken shells.

Shadows of a leg, an arm;
warm breeze and salt smell;
effortless birds.

Skimming stones,
seagulls air dance,
silent fisherman.

Experiment 6
Where am I?

1. Go to a place which is special to you. Open with your relaxing exercise (p. 16).
2. WALK through the area, and TOUCH or pick up five things. Each time, be aware of the contact of your hand with that surface or object.
3. Sit down and MAKE A LIST of 25 sensory specifics of the place you're in, trying for five sights, sounds, tastes, smells, textures.
4. If you like, read this list aloud to people, and ask them to guess the location. Ask which words give it away.

Did you notice
   —anything new about your favorite place?
   —whether you have more material from one or two senses than from others?
   —if you found just the right words to describe this setting and no other?

Experiment 7
Guess who's being described

This experiment is designed to sharpen your observation of details so that you can convey on paper the kind of image a photograph would capture. Aside from testing your ability to portray a person, you can use this experiment to create a character for a story.

1. CLIP A PICTURE of someone famous. Study his facial expression, build, hair, clothing.

2. CLOSE your eyes for a moment, and relax a little more with each outbreath. OPEN your eyes. Look at the picture. What strikes you first?

3. Write that as your first sentence. Continue describing this person from head to toe. Look at the picture often.

4. Try this with others: DESCRIBE someone in the room without naming the person. Write down ten words or phrases; list the most striking feature last.

5. READ your characterization aloud. How soon can others guess who's being described? Which words give it away?

Did you notice
 —*if you've written a "photographic" description?*
 —*what sort of details are more vivid and telling than others?*
 —*if facial expression, pose, or clothing suggest to you a story about this person? can you write the first paragraph now?*

Experiment 8
Sketch someone without explaining

You can use this experiment to make up a main character and begin a story.

1. MAKE a list of 15 words or phrases describing yourself. Begin with height, weight, build, hair, and go on to jobs you've had, places you've been, likes and dislikes, typical remarks.

19

2. MAKE another list like this for someone you know or would like to write about, or someone you create who could star in a story.

3. CHOOSE or MAKE UP one striking personality trait for your character, and write it out. Such as:
    Joel made jokes to cover up his shyness.
    Adele thought she wanted money more than anything.

4. CLOSE your eyes, for a moment, and picture your character in motion, walking out of the house, or into a party or board meeting. What does she notice first? What does she do? Can you see the expression on her face? What's she like with others?

5. OPEN your eyes. WRITE the first page of the story. BEGIN by describing your character going somewhere or arriving. DRAMATIZE her main trait so you see and hear her. Show how she's feeling through her:
    —walk (determined stride, or hesitating?)
    —posture (slouching, or standing tall?)
    —gesture (cigarette poised, or hands waving as she talks?)
    —tone of voice (whining, or authoritarian?)
    —clothing (starched, or top button open?)
    —facial expression (knitted brows, or beaming?).
    SHOW, rather than explain.

Did you notice
    —whether you know your character well? Could you see and hear her once you set her in motion?

SHAPING WHAT COMES

DESCRIBING A PLACE

You have written down many sensory details of a particular location, perhaps in the form of a list or a free-flow passage. What's most striking about this place, if you had to single out one thing? What first caught your eye? What main impression would you like to convey. (Do you have a story in mind that could happen in this setting?) Once you decide on a certain mood, you can select the details you need from all you wrote.

For instance, you're describing a room, and you want it to seem elegant. You'd include details such as polished teak floors, gold doorknobs, filigreed tables, but omit yellowing drapes. If you intend to give the impression of "elegant-but-fading," you could use all those details.

Obvious ways of picturing a place are from a physical point of view, that is, from left to right, top to bottom, focal point to periphery, near to far (or the reverse of any of these). Zoom in like a camera. First, the front of the house, the fence, the walk, the porch, the front door, the entrance hall, the stairs.

There's another way to tie together details. Your strong feeling about a setting would lend unity to a more "impressionistic" portrayal. Perhaps you wrote what struck you first, what thoughts stirred, what something reminded you of. If you're imagining a messy room, for instance, perhaps you don't want to write an orderly (right to left) description. Or, if you're trying to build suspense, you might send your imagination down a dark hallway and have a bat suddenly fly out. The point is: what works? What effect do you want to create, and does this arrangement of sentences bring out that feeling?

Here's an "impressionistic" description of a sunset walk on a Cape Cod beach, a moment of wonder:

Walking the beach, sensing each foot on the sand as sea blue crashes. White water in scallop pattern across the hard brown flats. Sunset reds concentrate in one small fish-scale cloud to the left, while to the right, the round red moon, big as a balloon, rises over the Atlantic. With each step, connecting bone and beach, feeling the pull of gravity. Air moves in and out. Rosy clouds sit on the grass-tipped dunes. A breeze picks up: cool touch on forehead, lifting strands of hair. The moon, striated like Mars, rises higher. Glinting waves, the widening path of light, clouds speeding by! And in the flood of moonlight, the starry world opening. . . .

21

Read aloud what you have: listen for the sound of it. How can you help the material find its form?

Write your experience as it happened; it may be just the order you want. Cross out anything which obviously detracts from the strong single impression you're making. Can you see and feel something about this place?

To sum up, when you shape your description:

1. Discover the main impression you want to create.

2. Or decide on the main feeling you have to convey.

3. Arrange sensory specifics to make the description build.

4. Cross out any details that don't contribute to your main impression.

5. Read aloud. Does this place come alive? Title your piece, and type it up.

NOW, WHAT COULD HAPPEN HERE?

Try another version of your description. Imagine this place while something's going on. A spaceship lands! A fire starts smoldering, then flares up. Two lovers enter. A man running. Write nonstop and see what happens.

If you're writing a story, try one more version of your piece. You can EXPRESS THE MOOD OF A CHARACTER by bringing out details of the environment. For instance, if you've just been praised or given a lot of money, and you're well-fed with nothing hurting at the moment, you might see the world as a shiny wonderful place. You might use any of the following details if asked to evoke a crowded street corner: sunlit, bright, smiling faces, smell of chestnuts roasting, shiny clothes, people bustling with life. That same corner, when you're tired or you just got yelled at, might suggest these words: glaring, loud, jostled, frowns, over-dressed, too much make up, zombies, chill wind, treeless. How subjectively we see the world at any moment! So if your main character is "in a state," select from all the descriptive details of a place just those which reflect his "inner landscape" as well.

Try this: CONVEY THE MOOD of a character by how he sees this place you've described. Add or alter details of what he perceives to suggest how he feels.

For example: —a boy walking home sees only what's dirty.
        —a man waits nervously.
        —a girl feels lonely since her boyfriend left.
        —she's exhausted after a fight with him.
        —you sold your first book!
        —he just helped deliver his first child.
        —she's got a crush on the new teacher.

Make up your own character and situation, then try creating a locale from his point of view. Does the world look beautiful or hostile? What thoughts interject themselves? Write nonstop the first page of a story. What could happen next? Keep going until something is resolved.

DESCRIBING A PERSON

How does he or she look, sound, smell, walk, eat, dress, walk? What strikes you first? Strength? Sexiness? What gives that impression?

Also, if you're creating a character for a story, what qualities about her fascinate? Think of favorite characters in books or films: what traits appeal? Good-natured humor? Persistence in the face of obstacles?

Your portrayal could focus on one main feature and include many sensory details. Using the material you've generated:

1. Make a note of what one strong characteristic impresses you.

2. Select details of appearance which stand out.

3. Show this person doing something typical or revealing: walking, talking to a friend, busy working at something.

4. Cross out items which don't add to the impression you're creating.

5. Does this person come alive? Can you see him? Type up.

You can weave in background information even as you give vivid sensory details. Here's an example from W. Somerset Maugham's novel *The Razor's Edge* (1949). English interior decorator Gregory Brabazon visits a rich American family, the Bradleys. Can you see him in their garish drawing room?

Gregory Brabazon, notwithstanding his name, was not a romantic creature. He was a short, very fat man, as bald as an egg except for a ring of black curly hair round his ears and at the back of his neck, with a red naked face that looked as though it were on the point of breaking out into a violent sweat, quick gray eyes, sensual lips and a heavy jowl. He was an Englishman and I had sometimes met him at bohemian parties in London. He was very jovial, very hearty and laughed a great deal, but you didn't have to be a great judge of character to know that his noisy friendliness was merely cover for a very astute man of business. He had been for some years the most successful decorator in London. He had a great booming voice and little fat hands that were wonderfully expressive. With telling gestures, with a spate of excited words he could thrill the imagination of a doubting client so that it was almost impossible to withhold the order he seemed to make it a favour to accept....

. . . I caught the professional look he gave the room as he came in and the involuntary lifting of his bushy eyebrows. It was indeed an amazing room. The paper on the walls, the cretonne of the curtains and on the upholstered furniture were of the same pattern; on the walls were oil paintings in massive gold frames that the Bradleys had evidently bought when they were in Rome. Virgins of the school of

Raphael, Virgins of the school of Guido Reni, landscapes of the school of Zuccarelli, ruins of the school of Pannini. There were trophies of their sojourn in in Peking, blackwood tables too profusely carved, huge cloisonné vases, and there were the purchases they had made in Chile or Peru, obese figures in hard stone and earthenware vases. There was a Chippendale writing table and a marquetry vitrine. The lampshades were of white silk on which some illadvised artist had painted shepherds and shepherdesses in Watteau costumes. It was hideous and yet, I don't know why, agreeable. It had a homely, lived-in air and you felt that that incredible jumble had a significance. All those incongruous objects belonged together because they were part of Mrs. Bradley's life.

You'll notice that this description says something about Brabazon, the Bradleys, and the narrator as well.

Chapter 2
Showing What Happened

These next experiments open wide the floodgates! People like them because they generate interesting writing painlessly. Often one taps a flow, strikes a rich vein.

In Experiment 9, for example, you'll invite an intense moment from your life (walking by the ocean, climbing a mountain, looking at the Acropolis, being frightened, getting caught stealing, falling in love). You could try to recall such a time, but it's not easy. Will a journey through the body bring back an instant in all its vividness?

Perhaps such memories are "locked" in muscle and tissue. One woman reported that relaxing her knees brought a flood of childhood memories about a drowning incident she had forgotten. Another woman imagined herself sitting in the Athenian marketplace, her back against a tree, talking to a pupil of Socrates: she wrote a story from the material.

What comes may surprise you, too.

You can direct yourself once you've tried these experiments, but for the first time it's useful just to let yourself go into the experience: have someone read the script while you relax with eyes closed. Try these at home with a friend helping you (but not when you're tired, or you'll fall asleep).

These next experiments are especially for people who want to free some fresh material for stories.

Experiment 9
Invite intense moments

Do this with a friend directing you (and others if you like). Find a carpeted quiet room. If you need to mask sounds, play music softly in the background (the second movement of Beethoven's Sixth works well). Keep a notebook and pen ready by your side.

Your "guide" will elaborate on these steps:

1. LIE DOWN on your back.

2. CLOSE YOUR EYES, and RELAX your face and body, moving down slowly from head to toe.

3. "GO" to a place where you've had an INTENSE MOMENT, and watch what happens there.

4. RETURN, open your eyes slowly, sit up, and WRITE NONSTOP what happened from beginning to end.

INSTRUCTIONS AND SCRIPT FOR YOUR GUIDE

Speak in a soothing quiet voice. Relax your body along with the experimenter(s) so you don't hurry. If there's background music, be sure it plays very quietly. Read aloud the parts in quotation marks (" "). Dots (. . .) mean to *pause*. Instructions for you are given in brackets [ ]. Tell your experimenter(s) to put pads and pens close by.

1. *"LIE DOWN on your back. Let the whole weight of your body sink into the floor. . . . Now you're beginning to relax. Starting with the top of your head, let a wave of relaxation sweep down your body. Your forehead relaxes. . . .*

2. *"RELAX your face . . . around the eyes. . . . Your jaw relaxes . . . your neck. . . .*
   [*Continue moving slowly down, naming out loud each part of the body, and suggesting it relax.*]

3. *"NOW, like an actor summoning a past experience, 'GO' to a place where you've had an intense moment. . . . You felt something powerful. . . . Where are you? . . . What colors? . . . What do you hear? . . .*

28

WATCH yourself *MOVE* through the scene to the end.
[*Wait at least 5 minutes before continuing.*]

4. *"When you're ready, you can come back to this room. . . . Very slowly, allow your eyes to open. . . . Sit up. . . . Pick up your pad and pen, and write as fast as you can to get it all down. Tell what happened from beginning to end. Go!"*
[*You can continue to use music to aid the flow of words, but keep it in the background.*]

(Note to guide: While others are writing, why not try Exp. 1?)

Did you notice
—*which of your senses were stirred during this experience? have you conveyed all those vivid sensory details?*
—*where in your writing there's a sense of something building?*
—*did you learn something about life? could you use this material in an autobiographical essay?*
—*if you have a setting for a story here or a possible main character in some emotional state?*

If no guide is available, and you want to recall intense moments, write across the top of the page one of the following:

> *One day I finally . . .*
> *Did this ever happen to you?*
> *My moment of truth came when . . .*

Then do your relaxing exercise (p. 16), and write nonstop.

* * *

The next experiment, "Travel through Time," brings out unusual writing and sometimes startling experiences. Some people find themselves "in a different body" moving through a place they've never been. And yet they can recapture it all in such detail!

29

One woman saw herself as a young boy holding his mother's hand as they walked toward an island village. She used this material as a dream sequence in a story she was writing about a woman who felt her parents always wanted a son not a daughter.

Another girl found herself flying over the ocean, seeing the cliffs of the continent, and landing in a German valley she had known as a young child, where she followed a path to a mysterious miller's cottage.

One woman saw herself as a cave-dweller in the future, working with tools, understanding a new language.

All these sketches developed into stories or essays.

Whatever your experience, your description will be vivid, with a quality of immediacy that's engaging. You'll be in control of your "travels" even as you watch them unfold, and when asked a question about them, will respond out loud without diminishing the experience.

Experiment 10
Travel through time[1]

Your guide will tell you these steps:

1. LIE DOWN on your back, CLOSE your EYES, and relax from head to toe.

2. VISUALIZE stretching out through the soles of your feet and the top of your head as if your body is getting longer; "expand all over" like a balloon.

3. PICTURE your house from the roof looking down, and then go higher so you can see the neighborhood. "TRAVEL."

4. "Land" on solid ground, feet first, and NOTICE what's around and how you're dressed.

5. When ready, sense your back on the floor, open your eyes, and WRITE free-flow every detail of what happened.

---

[1] This experiment was inspired by a procedure described in William Glaskin's fascinating book *Windows of the Mind* (New York: Delacorte Press).

SCRIPT FOR YOUR GUIDE

—If you want to mask outside noises, play softly a tape of Beethoven's *Pastoral*, 2nd movement, and Aaron Copland's "Corral Nocturne" (from *Rodeo*), or any quiet *background* music.

—Dots . . . mean to pause. Brackets [ ] enclose instructions for the guide.

—Tell experimenter(s) to sit on the floor with pad and pen close by. Mention that during the experiment you will ask a question, and the experimenter should respond out loud with a yes or no when requested. Explain that doing so will give the experimenter the feeling of being in control even while watching what unfolds.

1. *"LIE DOWN on your back . . . close your eyes. Allow all of your weight to sink into the floor. . . . Starting at the top of your head, a wave of relaxation flows down your body. Relax your forehead . . . around the eyes . . . your cheeks . . . your ears . . . your jaw relaxes. . . . [Continue moving down, suggesting each part relax.]*

2. *"Now VISUALIZE your feet as you lie here. Imagine them growing out six inches through the bottoms, as if your body has become longer by six inches. . . . [Ask out loud and wait for an answer:] Can you stretch six inches through your feet? Answer yes if you can. . . . Now focus on the top of your head. . . . Stretch out six inches through there, as if you are six inches longer. . . . [Ask out loud and wait for an answer:] Can you stretch out through the top of your head? Answer yes when you can. . . . Now expand all over, like a balloon, front and back, top and bottom and sides. . . . Now, you're ready to travel.*

3. *"PICTURE standing on the roof of your house, looking down at it. Notice details of your home from that angle, and notice the surrounding area. . . . Go up higher, so you can see the whole neighborhood. Whatever time of day it is, put the scene in full daylight. . . . You're in control of what you're seeing. Are you able*

31

to place the scene in full sunlight? Answer yes aloud if you can. [Wait for a response.] Notice that you still can sense your back on the floor even as you look at the landscape below. Now slowly turn in a complete circle over the building. . . . Go higher, and turn a wider circle. . . . Now the landscape is far below, and you begin to TRAVEL across the surface of the planet, watching what passes below. . . . [Pause a minute.]

4. *"Look for solid ground and come down feet first on a dry spot. . . . Glance at your feet: Are you barefoot? What are you wearing on them? . . . Look around. What's it like? . . . Any people? . . . Look down at your body. What are you wearing? Are you male or female? Young or old? . . . Begin walking. Is there a road? . . . How do you feel? . . . Any people? . . . What language do they speak? . . . What season is it? What year? . . . Keep walking. What do you see? . . . Hear? . . . Smell? . . . Follow where the path leads, noticing everything you can. . . . [Allow five minutes.]*

5. *"When you're ready to return, sense your back against the floor. Listen for the sounds of this room. Sense the length of your body on the floor. . . . Slowly open your eyes, and sit up. . . . Take your pad and pen, and WRITE NONSTOP getting down every detail from beginning to end."*

Or try the following variation of Experiment 10, based on a technique used by psychologists.

Experiment 10A
Travel through time and pick an era that attracts you

Your guide will tell you these steps:

1. LIE DOWN on your back, close your eyes, and relax.

2. As time periods are named, one will attract you, and you'll be able to "SEE" who you were then.

3. RETURN and write nonstop describing where you were, how you were dressed, and then telling what happened.

SCRIPT FOR YOUR GUIDE

Have experimenter(s) put pad and pen next to them on the floor. Instruct your experimenter(s) to answer yes or no when asked to respond out loud.

1. *"LIE DOWN on your back, and let the floor support the whole weight of your body. . . . Close your eyes, and allow your body to relax from head to toe. . . . Your face relaxes, around the eyes, your jaw, your throat relaxes. . . . [Continue moving slowly down the body, suggesting each part relax as you name it.]*

2. *"I'm going to call out five time periods. As I name a year, you may get a visual impression of yourself in that era. If you are attracted to a certain period, stay there. Look around. Notice what you're wearing. As I name years, stick with the one that brings you a vivid impression. See yourself there in a quiet ordinary moment when you're doing some simple activity. We'll begin now. [Pause 10 seconds between each date.]*
   1000 B.C. . . . 50 A.D. . . . 1150 . . . 1600 . . . 1850 . . . You're there. What are you wearing on your feet? . . . What kind of clothes? . . . Everything's quiet, and you're doing what? . . . Can you see yourself there? Answer yes out loud if you can. [Wait for a response.] Do you know that you're in control and can return whenever you want? Answer yes out loud. [Wait for a response.] Now watch yourself move through this place, noticing everything around you. . . . [Allow 5 minutes before continuing.]

3. *"You're ready to return to the present now. You can sense your back on the floor here, you're aware of your arms and legs, you can hear the sounds in this room. . . . Slowly open your eyes. . . . Sit up. . . . Pick up your pen and pad, and WRITE NONSTOP telling*

what happened from beginning to end. Keep your pen moving, letting all the details come out onto the page."

Did you notice
- *—a quality of immediacy and vividness in your account?*
- *—if you could begin a story with this material? or do you have a flashback or dream sequence for a story?*
- *—if at some point you felt you were about to discover something?*
- *—how much material you have access to when you explore in a new way? do you feel there's more you could tap?*

Experiment 11
Take a bird's-eye view[2]

Your guide will tell you these steps:

1. LIE DOWN, close your eyes, let tensions drain down and out.

2. IMAGINE your body getting denser, heavier, like a rock . . . and then more porous, lighter, like a feather.

3. CHANGE shape, grow wings, like a bird.

4. "FLY" to music.

5. Return, open your eyes, and WRITE NONSTOP describing your flight.

SCRIPT FOR YOUR GUIDE

For this experiment light flowing music is essential. Choose a piece which evokes the outdoors, such as "Lever du Jour" from Ravel's *Daphnis and Chloe.* Turn it on after step 4.

---

[2] Based on suggestions in Masters & Houston's *Mind Games* (Delta, 1972).

Instruct experimenter(s) to put pads and pens next to them on the floor and:

1. *"LIE DOWN on your back, and close your eyes. Let your face relax . . . and allow a wave of relaxation to flow down your body, relaxing face, jaw, neck. [Continue down the body, slowly, naming each part and suggesting relaxation.] Let the floor support the whole weight of your body.*

2. *"Your body is getting heavier now, denser, like rock. . . . You can feel it getting lighter, more porous, as if there's more space inside. Instead of rock, you're lighter, like wood. And getting lighter, more porous, like a feather floating just above the floor. . . . Now you feel the air on your skin. You're porous; it's as if the air can move right through you. . . .*

3. *"You see how you can become denser, and then more porous. You can be any size and shape, even another life form. Now visualize changing shape, getting smaller . . . your arms become wings . . . you have a beak . . . and you're taking the form of a bird. . . . Are you a robin? . . . An eagle? . . . Sense the air against your body. It's as if it lifts you, you're getting lighter, you can float just above the floor. . . . A breeze blows in through the open window, and now you can fly right out of this room. . . .*

4. *"You're above this building now, and can see the roof . . . you're rising higher . . . notice the landscape below . . . what do you see? . . . where are you flying to? . . . Let the music take you. . . . [Turn on MUSIC. Allow five minutes. Decrease volume just before speaking again.]*

5. *"When you're ready, you can return to your normal size and shape, sense your back on the floor here in this room. . . . Allow your eyes to open slowly, sit up. . . . Take pen and pad, and SKETCH IN WORDS your flight from beginning to end in any form. Write free-flow or let the experience unfold in phrases or*

images; write one on each line, like a poem." [*Put music on again, from the beginning, quietly as background.*]

Did you notice
—*if you've written part of an animal fable, and could add a moral?*
—*if you have the last paragraph for a story, giving the impression that your heroine has transcended something and is open now to new possibilities?*
—*you can use this material in your story to convey your character's dreams or fears or aspirations?*
—*how music can suggest vivid details of a place?*
—*whether this material lends itself to poetry or prose? could you write a poem? a dream sequence for a story?*

Experiment 12
Descend a dream stairway[3]

Your guide will tell you these steps:

1. LIE DOWN, CLOSE your EYES, let tensions drain down from head to toe and out of your body.

2. VISUALIZE yourself when you were ten years old.

3. REMEMBER a dream staircase at the back of the bedroom closet, and go down.

4. TRAVEL in a little boat, go ashore, look around.

5. Return and WRITE nonstop.

SCRIPT FOR YOUR GUIDE

Instruct experimenter(s) to put pad and pen close by.

1. "GET COMFORTABLE lying on your back on the floor, and allow your eyes to close. Let the floor sup-

---

[3] This experiment was inspired by a procedure described by Masters and Houston in *Mind Games*.

36

port your whole weight. . . . *RELAX your forehead,
and your face. . . . Let your jaw go limp . . . and your
neck. . . .* [*Move slowly down the body, suggesting that
each part relax or go limp, right to the toes.*]

2. "Now your body is getting smaller, shrinking to the
size it was when you were ten years old. . . . You can
see your hair . . . your arms and legs . . . chest . . .
your young face. . . .

3. "Now you can remember a dream you used to have as
a child. You're in bed. You get up and walk over to
the closet, and find that there's a door at the back, and
it opens. . . . There's a staircase of stone, and you're
eager to go down it . . . you go step by step. . . . You
look around . . . you hear water lapping. . . .

4. "At the bottom of the stairs, there's a little boat. You
get in, and sit down on the blankets. . . . The boat
rocks gently and begins moving toward some light
ahead. . . . You go out through the opening, and
you're in full sunlight, drifting downstream . . . the
sun warms your face. . . . Look at the shoreline . . .
smell the air, notice its coolness on your skin. . . .
There's a meadow. . . . You float ashore, and get out
of the boat . . . the grass touches your legs . . . it's
beautiful . . . head for that big tree . . . run up to it,
and sit down in its shade. . . . Glance around. . . .
How do you feel? . . . Take it all in . . . contented . . .
peaceful. . . . Off in the distance you see something
. . . what is it? . . . Do you want to go there? . . . Follow where you want to go. . . . [Allow five minutes.]

5. "Whenever you're ready, you can return to this room.
Your body takes its usual shape, and you can sense
your back on the floor. . . . Listen to the sounds in this
room. . . . Allow your eyes to open slowly . . . and
sit up. WRITE NONSTOP and tell what you saw and
what happened from beginning to end." [*Optional: put
on some soft flowing music in the background.*]

Did you notice
    —if each of your senses was engaged at some point?

37

—how you can have access to "dream" material if you relax first in this way?

—if there's an opening for a story here? a fairy tale? or could this material be a flashback?

Experiment 13
Listen in—How do people talk?

1. MAKE A STUDY of how people talk.
   a. Watch TV with the sound off and notice postures, gestures, facial expressions that accompany emotion. Can you guess what's being said and felt?
   b. Pick one person you meet today, and when he talks, particularly notice body language, the position of that person's arms, also facial expressions. Do you ever get a "double message" (when gestures or a look seem to say the opposite of the words coming out)? Notice tone of voice—how would you label it?
   c. Walk past public phones, and eavesdrop: catch bits of conversation and record these in a notebook. (If these snatches suggest a poem to you, create one from this material.)[4]

2. (Optional, but recommended if you can find a group to work with who also want to make this study.)

   THINK UP A CHARGED SITUATION (perhaps the one in your story-to-be?), and have two people spontaneously play out a scene. Just get one person to start talking, and the conversation will get going. As you observe, notice gestures, intonation, facial expression; become aware of how dialogue sounds when it rings true.

   Some sample scenes might be:
   a. After 30 years of marriage, she finds the nerve to ask him for a divorce. He just got off the golf course. She begins, "John, it's time we had a little talk."

---
[4] Step C. was suggested by David Applebaum.

b. She wants to break off the engagement but won't tell him why. "I have to go now, Peter."

c. She wants to get a job, and he wants her to iron his "lucky shirt" for tomorrow's big meeting. She might respond, "Is that all I can do? Iron your shirts?"

d. Re-play situations a, b, or c but try NOT TO ARGUE. Each person tries to stand in the other's shoes, be understanding, help the other to be happy.

3. MAKE A STUDY OF YOUR OWN BODY when you're afraid, angry, depressed, or excited. ACT OUT a "charged moment."

a. You're about to appear on live TV for the first time. Visualize yourself waiting to go on, and take that position. Scan your body from head to toe: How is your stomach? Fluttery? How about your breathing? Heartbeat? Pulse? Is one foot moving nervously?

b. You slam down the receiver of the telephone. You're furious! What do you do? What's the expression on your face? Jaw tight? Pound on something? Kick over something?

c. You're depressed and you can't stop worrying. How are you sitting? Slumped? Playing with a strand of hair? Moist around the eyes? A lump or knot in your throat?

4. Picture your main character TALKING TO SOMEONE about something that means a lot. CLOSE your EYES for a few minutes, and really visualize this meeting. Something's coming to a head, or something's about to be revealed! Watch the two talking, gesturing; see their faces.

OPEN your EYES and WRITE THAT SCENE. What's the situation? If you have only a general idea, start writing anyway, beginning with a question such as X saying: "What have you got to tell me that's so important?" or: "Why have you come here?" Let each line prompt the next.

Did you notice
—how body language can speak louder than words?

—that has force, and a direct question demands a response?

—how dramatic and fascinating the interaction between people can be? how dialogue holds your attention?

—how you can verify, in your own body, appropriate postures and gestures for certain emotional states?

Experiment 14
Imagine a crisis moment—what happens?

Try this at the shore, or by a stream or river.

1. Sit outdoors, and open with your relaxing exercise (p. 16).

2. When you SLOWLY OPEN your EYES, what strikes you first? WRITE that sensory detail in a sentence.

3. IMAGINE your main character waiting here. Something's about to happen, a feeling is building in her, someone's coming any minute—

4. And it happens! WRITE NONSTOP who or what comes, what's said, what's resolved.

5. Something's over now—or has just begun! To conclude, use a sensory detail (like the one you wrote down in step 2) to convey a feeling about this place and what occurred. Your last words might be "Two gulls crisscrossed above her, and with a cry were gone."

Did you notice
—how your imagination can take over once you open to a place and have the idea that something's about to happen there?
—that sensory details, rather than an explanation, can convey a powerful moment of experience?
—whether what you see depends on how you're feeling?

40

SHAPING WHAT COMES

You can build a story from the material you've generated doing Experiments 1, 3, 6–14. Here are some of the ways people take what they write free-flow and let it stimulate them to write more.

1. Read all you've written. UNDERLINE parts you like, especially sentences which suggest the GERM of a story. It may be the vivid recollection of a past moment, or just an account of a person feeling a particular way in a special place. Start from there.

2. Make up a MAIN CHARACTER (try Exp. 8, p. 19), perhaps modeled after someone you know. Name him or her. Put that name, and *he* or *she*, instead of *I* in your writings.

   Does any of it suggest a story yet? What could be his problem? Her situation? How is he feeling and why? Imagine what might happen next.

3. Combine material from different experiments. Your main character is sitting on a hillside, closes his eyes, and suddenly he flashes back in time. What's about to happen to him?

4. Locate exciting moments in your writing, sudden movements, and interactions between people. Begin a new paragraph each time you shift gears.

   Don't worry about material which seems extra or doesn't fit. Put brackets [ ] around it.

5. NOW TRY TO WRITE JUST ONE PAGE, ANY PAGE, of your story.

   If several "scenes" suggest themselves and you don't know what to write first, start with the one you know you can write now—and put it on paper in any form. *Don't worry about your first sentence,* just get going. Later you'll sense where this material will fit. You may end up writing your opening last.

6. Are you at a point where you could put in some *dialogue*? Write nonstop one page or more. Who does she meet? Who could he talk to? What's the *conflict*?

7. Can you say yet what this story's about? Try it out loud in 25 words or less. "This story's about a young woman who. . . ." Good! You've discovered your *theme*.

8. If the rest of the story is clear to you, make some notes about what happens. Then jot down whatever part you can now, even if it's just a paragraph. Or write it all!

9. When you have many sections of the story, put them in order. Which should come first? How do you want to introduce your character and the situation?

Create a first draft of your story, using all the sections you've composed, weaving them together so something builds. Reread the first line of some of your favorite stories: do you jump right in? Does it take too long to lead into the action?

For your present story, should you begin with dialogue? Description? Bring out some conflict? Resolve it by having something climactic happen that affects the main character?

Your story may not fit that model: it may have taken a shape all its own. If you're looking for a framework, though, here's a summary of one approach to organizing your material.

FOUR STEPS FOR STORY WRITERS

1. *Discover your main character.*
Then start him out right in the middle of some activity or just before something is going to happen. With

vivid sensory details, show him in action in a particular place.

2. *Place your character in conflict.*
   What's the situation? What's her problem? Is something about to occur? Who else is involved?
   Conflict means opposing forces, potential fireworks. Have the situation "heat up" through:
   > *dialogue* (include posture, gesture, tone of voice, facial expression), and
   > *description* (convey your character's state of mind by how he sees his surroundings).

   Whenever possible, SHOW rather than explain. (Instead of "He was frightened," describe heartbeat, perspiration, breathing, or behavior.)

   TENSION'S BUILDING. Conflict keeps things in motion, so the action "rises" to some intense moment.

3. *Move swiftly to the crisis,* turning point, or "moment of truth."

   What happens? What's resolved? Which, if any, of the opposing forces triumphs? How is your character different now?

   Stop once the action's over to avoid going on too long after the climax.

4. *Edit out parts that slow down the story.*

   Where does the narrative drag? Does the action get lost in too many words? Is your language too flowery (strings of adjectives)? Is any legal or business jargon creeping in where not appropriate?

   As an experiment, try cutting out every extra word you can find. Is it better? *Do events move swiftly to create a strong single impression?*

   FIND A TITLE that's engaging but not overdone. Type up your final draft. Good for you!

Part 4 (Toward Becoming Your Own Best Editor) can help you tighten and sharpen your writing.

Rather than worrying about impressing a reader, please only yourself. Chances are if your writing rings true for you, someone else will be touched by it.

WRITING AN AUTOBIOGRAPHICAL ESSAY

You've had a powerful experience that taught you something. Perhaps it's come out in your free-flow writing. You wonder whether it might become the germ of an article or essay.

What's your purpose in writing the piece? Do you want to:

—entertain?
—inform?
—comment on human nature?
—re-live, explore, or understand something?
—instruct yourself through your writing?
—get excited?
—have an adventure?

Fine! When you speak from experience, you create a feeling of shared intimacy. Be confident that when you write in vivid detail what you've lived, it'll reach someone who's felt the same thing.

Showing what happened is not reserved for fiction alone. A pertinent incident or conversation will liven up and make a strong point in any essay. You can follow the chronological order of events as they happened, or begin just before a moment of realization. Try flashing back or forward in time. Dialogue will make your examples come alive.

To sum up:

1. WHAT LESSON about life, people, or yourself did you learn from an intense moment you recalled? SAY IT out loud in a sentence. Use that as your opening, or as your final sentence.

2. ILLUSTRATE that lesson with one or more examples, an incident or conversation you recreate. Write each example in a paragraph. If you use

several moments, save the most dramatic or telling illustration for last.

3. CONCLUDE at the moment of greatest emotional impact. End with a sentence or two that tells just how you felt, and what the moment taught you. No need to embellish: say it in plain English.

Here's an example. In the autobiographical essay "Shame," Dick Gregory recalls incidents in school and on the streets that made him feel ashamed when he was growing up in the slums. He records painful exchanges in class with his teacher, and his refusal to wear the same plaid mackinaw as 3000 other "welfare boys." But the thing that taught him most about "shame" he saves for last. He relates an incident which took place in a restaurant. Gregory was eating when a wino came in:

The old wino sat down at the counter and ordered twenty-six cents worth of food. He ate it like he really enjoyed it. When the owner, Mister Williams, asked him to pay the check, the old wino didn't lie or go through his pocket like he suddenly found a hole.

He just said: "Don't have no money."

The owner yelled: "Why in hell you come in here and eat my food if you don't have no money? That food cost me money."

Mister Williams jumped over the counter and knocked the wino off his stool and beat him over the head with a pop bottle. Then he stepped back and watched the wino bleed. Then he kicked him. And he kicked him again.

I looked at the wino with blood all over his face and I went over. "Leave him alone, Mister Williams. I'll pay the twenty-six cents."

The wino got up, slowly, pulling himself up to the stool, then up to the counter, holding on for a minute until his legs stopped shaking so bad. He looked at me with pure hate. "Keep your twenty-six cents.

45

You don't have to pay, not now. I just finished paying for it."

He started to walk out, and as he passed me, he reached down and touched my shoulder. "Thanks, sonny, but it's too late now. Why didn't you pay it before?"

I was pretty sick about that. I waited too long to help another man.

What did he learn about shame? Do you see and feel any of what he did? Notice the last two sentences: what makes them effective?

Whether you want to do a story or an essay, think about it, plan, but START WRITING—even a page! More ideas will come *while* you're putting words on paper. If you get stuck, find a part that you could write now: there's usually some description or dialogue you can get into. Build momentum by writing nonstop again and again.

ABOUT WRITING DIALOGUE

"Oh, please. . . ."

"Forget it!"

What's happened between these two? Want to find out? Give the speakers names, and write the rest of the conversation.

Dialogue is easy to take in, and engaging. Even an ordinary report can be enlivened by quoting. A person's voice has a directness and immediacy that says a lot about a situation.

If you know your characters well enough, you understand their views on everything and how they'll react. (What would Groucho say when a pretty girl comes into the room?)

For dialogue that rings true, try the following, where appropriate. Then read out loud what you wrote.

1. Use contractions (I've, don't, you've).

2. Try slang expressions that fit the age and upbringing of your character.

3. Use direct questions, with question marks, to provoke a response.

4. When beginning, be sure to indicate who's speaking (so there are no disembodied voices).

5. Did you overuse "he said" (wheezed, shouted, retorted)? Here are ways to indicate who's speaking:

a. Begin a new paragraph (indent 5 spaces) each time the speaker changes.

If only two people are talking, see if it's clear who's speaking without naming the person (for a few lines at least).

b. Have the person talk. Then within the same paragraph, follow with a sentence indicating her posture or movement, such as:

"Won't you sit down just for a minute?"
Sandra poured out two cups of coffee.

In the story below, respectable farmer Peter goes a little crazy when his wife dies; he begins to reveal embarrassing secrets to his neighbor Ed. Notice how dialogue and description strike a balance: "he said" is hardly used, but you know who's talking and can see him move and gesture. And you want to read on!

. . . Ed's hand went out toward the bromide bottle, but Peter shook his head.

"No need to give me anything, Ed. I guess the doctor slugged me pretty hard, didn't he? I feel all right now, only a little dopey."

"If you'll just take one of these, you'll get some sleep."

"I don't want to sleep." He fingered his draggled beard and then stood up. "I'll go out and wash my face, then I'll feel better."

Ed heard him running water in the kitchen. In a moment he came back into the living-room, still drying his face on a towel. Peter was smiling curiously. It was an expression Ed had never seen on him before, a quizzical, wondering smile. "I guess I kind of broke loose when she died, didn't I?" Peter said.

"Well—yes, you carried on some."

"It seemed like something snapped inside of me," Peter explained. "Something like a suspender strap. It made me come apart. I'm all right now, though."

Ed looked down at the floor and saw a little brown spider crawling, and stretched out his foot and stomped it.

Peter asked suddenly, "Do you believe in an after-life?"

Ed Chappell squirmed. He didn't like to talk about such things, for to talk about them was to bring them up in his mind and think about them. "Well, yes. I suppose if you come right down to it, I do."

"Do you believe that somebody that's—passed on —can look down and see what we're doing?"

"Oh, I don't know as I'd go that far—I don't know."

Peter went on as though he were talking to himself. "Even if she could see me, and I didn't do what she wanted, she ought to feel good because I did it when she was here. It ought to please her that she made a good man of me. If I wasn't a good man when she wasn't here, that'd prove she did it all, wouldn't it? I was a good man, wasn't I, Ed?"

"What do you mean, 'was'?"

"Well, except for one week a year I was good. I don't know what I'll do now. . . ." His face grew angry. "Except one thing." He stood up and stripped off his coat and his shirt. Over his underwear there was a web harness that pulled his shoulders back. He unhooked the harness and threw it off. Then he dropped his trousers, disclosing a wide elastic belt. He shucked this off over his feet, and then he scratched his stomach luxuriously before he put on his clothes again. He smiled at Ed, the strange, wondering smile, again. "I don't know how she got me to do things, but she did. She didn't seem to boss me, but she always made me do things. You know, I don't think I believe in an after-life. When she was

48

alive, even when she was sick, I had to do things she wanted, but just the minute she died, it was—why like that harness coming off! I couldn't stand it. It was all over. I'm going to have to get used to going without that harness." He shook his finger in Ed's direction. "My stomach's going to stick out," he said positively, "I'm going to let it stick out. Why, I'm fifty years old."

Ed didn't like that. He wanted to get away. This sort of thing wasn't very decent. "If you'll just take one of these, you'll get some sleep," he said weakly.

(from John Steinbeck's
"The Harness")

Use this, or any dialogue you read, as a model for setting up the conversation you write.

Look over the dialogue and note if it moves the story forward? Does something "heat up?" Is anything revealed?

Chapter 3
Explaining Something

How should you explore your subject?

You can ask yourself a question, or a series of questions, about it. Try interviewing people. You might read what others have written.

Here are some additional ways to help you discover your slant.

The Grafitti Game, for instance, is a great technique for getting into any area of discussion. Put a "hot issue," in a word or phrase, on a blackboard, and watch each person respond to it with another word or phrase that gives her slant. Soon someone reacts to that, and puts up another phrase. Watch your "group poster poem" grow, and with it, a sense of shared creativity.

Experiment 15
Play the Grafitti Game

There are three versions you can try, depending on circumstances. All will generate enthusiasm, the excitement of creating together with other people. This experiment can be tried even at a party—it gets everyone moving!

Two or twenty can play. The idea is to make something together with words and phrases, and watch your creation unfold. You can use a blackboard and chalk (white or colors). Or set up a large white poster or polymer board on the mantelpiece or on an easel, and have some colored magic markers ready. Or simply do this with one or two others writing in turn on a large pad.

Version 1. Write a "group poster poem":

1. To warm-up, have everyone write free-flow for five minutes (Exp. 1). First, assure the group they're not going to have to read aloud, that this part of the experiment is just to get going. Write: "NOW I'M SITTING HERE AND" across the top of a pad (each person should have his own pad and pencil). Put it aside, and sit quietly for a moment, letting the body relax, while listening to all the sounds in the room. Pick up the pen, complete that sentence, and keep writing nonstop. (Stress the importance of keeping the pen moving and talking on paper.) Go!

2. Have everyone read over their writing, and circle or underline phrases "that you like or that strike you."

3. On the poster or board, write: "NOW I'M STANDING HERE AND." Encourage someone to go up and add a sentence or phrase anywhere on the board in any kind of lettering. Encourage another person to add to it. Be patient until things get moving, and watch each addition to the group poem. When the space is covered, suggest that someone finish it. Enjoy what you've made together! Read it aloud.

Version 2. Explore any subject, concept, or word:

1. Put a word or phrase on the board which will be the "theme" or "subject" of exploration.

   (One group wanted to investigate attitudes about men and women. To begin, a person wrote HE on the right half and SHE on the left half of the board.)

2. Encourage participants to write words or phrases anywhere on the empty space, noting each person's addition before putting up another. When you feel you've explored all the angles, suggest that someone complete the group poster poem.

52

Version 3. Use different kinds of music or sound effects:

1. Select in advance a few different kinds of *instrumental* music, and together do one group poster poem to each piece.

   (Try a poem to Stockhausen's "Kontake" and see what electronic music suggests to the participants. Do another poster poem to a lilting classical piece. Or to the roar of the ocean.)

2. Erase the board or start with a clean sheet each time you complete a poster poem and change the music. Explore the various themes different sounds suggest.

Did you notice
   —*how words generate more phrases and ideas?*
   —*anything revealing about people's attitudes or beliefs?*
   —*interesting juxtapositions, or anything startling or clever? did some subjects call forth only stock and clichéd responses?*
   —*how music and free-flow writing stimulate writing?*
   —*a feeling of satisfaction, pride, or closeness develop in the group? or, just the opposite?*

Experiment 16
Find sensory specifics to illustrate ideas

---

1. If your subject is an abstract noun such as *shame, freedom, boredom, success*, write it at the left side of a blackboard, posterboard, or pad. Next to it, write these headings:

looks like?	sounds like?	smells like?	tastes like?	feels like to touch?

2. By yourself, or with others, fill in those columns. What does boredom look like? "A hundred tract houses." What does boredom sound like? "A dripping faucet," "a droning voice." Be as specific as you can. List *four* concrete sensory details for *each* heading. (If you're doing this with others, encourage rapid responses: it might take a few minutes to get the hang of it.)

3. Don't write down a word or phrase unless it's more specific than your original "idea" noun. That is, don't accept responses like *tedium* or *monotony* for "What does boredom look like?" Ask, "What does monotony look like?" until you get some specific detail you can perceive with your senses.

4. For more practice, erase the board or take a clean sheet, and write another abstract word onto it. Discover some new ways to describe some old feelings.

Did you notice
—*that you can find vivid sensory equivalents for nearly any "idea" word?*
—*that the more you try to find such specifics, the more occur to you?*
—*if it's easier to find sights and sounds than textures, tastes, or smells? that it is possible to find details which engage all the senses?*

Experiment 17
Contrast then and now

Version 1. Explore your attitudes about the sexes:

1. Write across the top of a page: "WHEN I WAS YOUNGER, I." Turn the page over and write across the top "I REMEMBER ONE TIME." Across the top of the third sheet write: "NOW I." You can try this yourself, or have a friend direct you.[1]

2. Open with your relaxing exercise (p. 16) done lying down.

3. PICTURE yourself as you were in junior high, at a school dance. What are you wearing? Look around. What are you feeling about the others there? Boys? Girls? Watch your movements as the scene unfolds. . . .

[1] NOTE TO YOUR GUIDE: Speak quietly, don't hurry. Allow two or three minutes before you read aloud each new step.

Imagine a first–time moment. Recall and return to an instant when you experienced something about the sexes for the first time. What happens? How do you feel? . . .

4. Open your eyes, pick up your pen, and WRITE NON-STOP completing the sentence. Do it quickly. When you turn the page and come to a new heading, go with that and keep your pen moving. Cover all three pages with words.
5. To supplement this material, INTERVIEW PEOPLE:

   a. TALK with your mother or father, asking, "What advice did you used to give me about (boys) (girls) (men) (women)?"
   b. TALK with a childhood pal or best friend. RE-CALL how you each felt about the opposite sex: can you remember an earlier incident or conversation? Did you have a stereotyped image of what men or women were like?
   c. WRITE FREELY NONSTOP: "When I was young, boys were. . . ." Or "When I was young, girls were. . . ." Let specific incidents from your experience make the writing come alive.

Here's a sample, from Anne Roiphe's "Confessions of a Female Chauvinist Sow." When she was younger, she wholeheartedly believed the stereotyped view of boys:

Boys were fickle and likely to be unkind; my mother and I knew that, as surely as we knew they tried to make you do things in the dark they wouldn't respect you for afterwards, and in fact would spread the word and spoil your rep. Boys like to be flattered; if you made them feel important they would eat out of your hand. So talk to them about their interests, don't alarm them with displays of intelligence—we all knew that, we groups of girls talking into the wee hours of the night in a kind of easy companionship we thought impossible with boys. Boys were prone to have a good time, get you pregnant, and then pretend they didn't know your name when you came knocking on their door for finances or comfort. In short, we believed boys were less moral than we were. They appeared to be hypocritical, self-seeking, exploitative, untrustworthy and very likely to be showing off their precious masculinity. I never had a girl friend I thought would be unkind or embarrass me in public. I never expected a girl to lie to me about her marks or sports skills or how good she was in bed. Altogether—without anyone directly coming out and saying so—I gathered that men were sexy, powerful, very interesting, but not very nice, not very moral, humane and tender, like us. . . .

d. To explore this area more deeply, try Experiment 20.

Version 2. Explore your ambitions:

1. Write across the top of the page: "WHEN I WAS YOUNGER, I WANTED." Write across the top of the other side "NOW I WANT." Across the top of a third sheet, write: "WHAT WILL I BE DOING TEN YEARS FROM NOW?" Have a friend direct you through these steps:

2. Lie down, and open with your relaxing exercise (p. 16).

3. PICTURE yourself at graduation. A classmate asks you, "So, what do you want to do with your life?" What do you tell her?

4. RELAX your body once more, sweeping down from head to toe. Try to PICTURE how you'll look ten years from now. . . . Where are you? Who are you with? What are you doing? Follow the scene as long as you can.

5. Open your eyes, pick up your pen, and write nonstop completing the sentence on the first page. When you come to the next heading, WRITE quickly from that point. Answer the question on the top of the third

page. Keep the pen moving, and see what comes as you talk on paper.

6. To supplement this material, INTERVIEW PEOPLE:
   a. TALK with a parent or relative, asking, "When I was young, what did you really think I'd turn out to be?"
   b. Ask an old friend, and then a new friend, "What do you think I'll be doing ten years from now?"

Did you notice
   —any surprises in what you wrote or what others said to you?
   —how earlier experiences affected your attitudes?
   —whether your views have changed, and in what ways?
   —that sometimes you don't know what you think until you see what you say on paper?
   —that writing can help you understand more clearly what you really feel?

Experiment 18
Do something, then tell "how-to"

Explain a procedure: try for one step (and no more) per sentence.

Version 1. To inform:

1. Write across the top of the page: "What do I know how to do that someone else would want to know how to do?"

2. Put aside pad and pen, and open with your relaxing exercise (p. 16).

3. WRITE nonstop by talking on paper for a page. UNDERLINE highlights. Decide what process you'll describe.

4. Write at the top of a page: "HOW TO *(your subject)*." Below, list step 1, step 2, step 3. . . .

57

5. TALK out each step, then write it down just that way.

6. Assume your reader knows nothing about this procedure.
   —Is each step clear? Small enough? Do you need to add another step just to help her follow more easily?
   —Are there terms your reader might not know? Explain them.
   —Any pitfalls she might encounter? Warn against common mistakes.
   —Do you raise, but not answer, any questions?

7. READ ALOUD to someone just to be sure you've got all the steps, with no gaps, or confusing parts. Ask your listener to tell you which part she needs to hear again.

8. WRITE an introductory sentence or two, perhaps opening with an ANECDOTE that tells what it was like the first time you tried to make a soûfflé, develop a photo, repair fiberglass.

Version 2. To entertain:

1. Make up an unlikely "how-to" title, then try to write a funny piece giving step-by-step tactics.

   To get going, make a LIST of titles. ASK FRIENDS to add to it.

   How to Bomb in Bed
   How to Expand Your Intelligence through Comic Books
   How to Get Rid of a Tan

   Choose the one that appeals to you most.

2. OPEN with reasons why someone would want to do this. Write as if you're serious. Exaggerate; pile it on. Highlight with examples or anecdotes you make up. Give steps 1, 2, 3. . . . (Even though you're not serious, is there a note of truth behind what you wrote? Some comment about how we are?)

3. READ ALOUD to people to see if and where they laugh or smile.

Did you notice
  —*how clear you have to be about a process before telling others? did explaining it make it clearer to you?*
  —*anything new about something you do automatically?*
  —*how to make a "how-to" piece funny?*
  —*if you kept to "one step, one sentence?"*

Experiment 19
Research a burning question

1. Do your opening exercise (p. 16).

2. You want to become an expert on a subject that really interests you. FILL IN this sheet:
   What really interests me? What do I want to know more about?
   1.
   2.
   3.
   4.

3. CHOOSE the most intriguing response, and write free-flow a few sentences, answering:
   —Specifically, what about it? What do I want to understand?
   —Write a few more sentences, or phrases, nonstop, answering: What could I find out?

4. Try to phrase what you are after in the form of a question with a question mark. Ask yourself the question you'll want to answer.[1]
   —How (What) (Why) (When) (Where) (Who) ——
   ————————————————?

---
[1] Such as, How did writing begin? What are the origins of golf? What are man's possibilities for development? Who holds the baseball record for the most . . . ? Where does electricity come from and where does it go? What's a quasar?

5. Go on a TREASURE HUNT and discover a wealth of material that'll make you an expert on this particular subject. Don't stop until you have your answer. WRITE YOUR QUESTION ON AN INDEX CARD or a sheet of paper, and carry it with you. Look at it often so you're clear about just what you need (and what you don't).

6. MAP out where you'll look for material, or follow these directions. With card and notebook, go to the LIBRARY.
   —Underline key words in your question, to guide you through card catalogues. What's your SUBJECT?
   —Check subject cards (arranged alphabetically) in the card catalogue, and write down the names and call numbers of BOOKS which might have what you need.
   —Check subject entries (also arranged alphabetically) in the *Reader's Guide to Periodical Literature* (this year's, or whatever year when articles might have been written about your subject), and copy down the names and volume and page for MAGAZINES which might contain what you need.
   —Ask the librarian if you're not sure where to look for these books and magazines.
   —Glance at your card again, then check through the INDEX at the back of each book. Photocopy pages with material you need, or make notes. Be sure to write down the book, author, publisher, city of publication, year of publication, and page numbers.
   —Skim magazine articles. Be sure to write down publishing information (titles, author, publication, volume, date, page) for each source you use.

7. You have gathered an abundance of material! Read over your notes, underline highlights. Do you have your answer yet? Find out by trying some free-flow writing. Do Experiment 28. Go on to Experiment 29 to come up with your first draft. If you need some suggestions for ways to shape your answer, see below.

Did you notice
 —*there's more to the answer than you thought?*
 —*your question got more specific as you researched it?*
 —*it's useful to work on something you really care to know about? that you stick to it, and enjoy finding answers?*
 —*anything exciting in your exploration which leads to other questions you might want to answer?*

SHAPING WHAT COMES

SIX WAYS TO EXPLAIN

Explaining something means telling what's what. You elaborate on the causes, results, stages, steps, reasons, types, relationships. You inform. Six common ways to explain are to:

1. illustrate with examples.
2. define.
3. discover the parts or types.
4. compare or contrast.
5. show how.
6. show why.

You can use combinations of these means of explanation as well.

For instance, you're writing about résumés. You classify the different kinds: "There are five kinds of résumés" and give an example of each.

Or you're writing about *revolution*. You define the word, using a dictionary, and then show how its meaning has changed over the years. Illustrate with examples from books, commercials, magazines.

Which means will help you organize your material for greatest impact? Here's a brief description of different ways to present the facts.

1. *Illustrate* with examples: show what something is.
   As you discovered from Experiment 16, sensory specifics create vivid pictures, and can help ideas come

alive. After writing an opening which gives your slant on a topic, illustrate your point with a series of telling examples. Save the "clincher" for last.

2. *Define:* tell what something is.
Some essays first define key terms so your reader knows just how you're using an important word. Don't take it for granted that the word *world* means the same thing to everyone: ask, and you'll get many definitions. A dictionary can help you set the bounds for the term you're using, place it in a class, give specific characteristics. Quote part of the entry as a way to introduce your subject.

3. *Discover the parts* of a whole: "Three are 3 kinds of . . ."
You researched a burning question and discovered the different aspects or parts of your subject, their relationship to each other and to the whole. You sort out, and arrange: what kinds or types exist? (Later you may want to contrast categories and illustrate with specifics.)

4. *Compare or contrast* (show what something is or is not like).
List qualities or characteristics shared by X and Y: these are your bases of comparison. For instance, both plants X and Y have roots; both flower, and need light. Roots, flowers, light: items 1, 2, and 3 you'll compare in detail for X and Y. Or contrast them: X and Y both have roots, *but* X's roots are shorter; both flower, *but* Y rarely yields fruits; they both need light, *but* Y thrives in the shade. You've shown how two things are alike and different. A fair comparison or contrast gives equal attention to X and Y, looking at item 1 for each, then item 2, then item 3. See Experiment 26, p. 108.

5. *Show how:* steps in a process.
Demonstrate how to do or how we do something by breaking the process into steps small enough so a reader can follow. Use one step as one sentence or

one paragraph. Give examples. If the process is complex, take a small part at a time, and sort out the main steps. Write "first," "second," "next."

6. *Show why:* causes and effects, problems and solutions. Your burning question may have led to discoveries about why and how something happened. You researched an event and traced its causes. You asked, "Why do . . . ?" Decide whether to move from causes to effects, or work back from effects to causes: which would be the stronger way to present your material? (Also, remember that just because something happened before something else, the first didn't necessarily *cause* the second.) Look for several causes, both immediate and remote. Did event A *result* in event B? You want to try to piece together the puzzle and give an accurate account of what happened.

If a particular problem interests you, consider it as an "effect" and discover its causes. They may lead you to possible solutions. Ask yourself, why did this happen and what can be done? (Talk out your answer on paper, nonstop, and see if some solutions come out.) Weigh the advantages and disadvantages (make lists) of possible solutions, so you can decide on the best answer. In your essay, state the problem, what brought it about, and suggest ways to deal with it. End on that strong note.

Experiments in the next chapter show how you can persuade your reader.

Chapter 4
Convincing Someone

What makes us listen to one person and not another?

Can you remember the last time someone convinced you of something? What did it take?

We want to trust the person speaking. Does he sound intelligent, fair, and reasonable? We'd like to respect the writer, and feel that he respects us.

What would keep a reader from sharing your views, accepting your reasoning, and taking the action you suggest? Perhaps she doesn't understand the ideas you're explaining: are you clear? Or, she doesn't like what's coming through: are you browbeating or talking down to your reader? Or, she doesn't think you're justified in saying what you do: have you presented enough evidence to validate your opinion?

Convincing someone takes the right balance of logic and emotion. If the reader feels you're humane, honest, sincerely searching for truth, she may go along with you. But first, do you believe what you're saying, and has it come out on the page as you'd like?

Experiments 20 and 21 are enjoyable ways to test your powers of persuasion.

Experiments 22 and 23 will help you practice writing letters with just the right tone to be effective.

Experiment 20
Give your views about men and women today

Try this first part[1] with others to get an impression of today's attitudes about *men* and *women*.

---

[1] Inspired by an activity suggested by Janaro & Gearhart, *Human Worth* (New York: Holt, Rinehart and Winston, Inc., 1973), p. 572.

1. DIVIDE into small groups, all-male, and all-female. Each group has to come up with a single LIST of ten characteristics of the ideal man, ranked from most important to least important. Make the most important number 1.

2. Each group then writes "the ideal *woman* is. . . ." List ten qualities, ranked from most important (number 1) to least important (number 10).

3. Collect the lists, and have someone read them randomly. After each list is read, can you guess whether it characterizes a woman or man? Was it written by a men's or women's group? How do you know? Is any one list very different from the others? Any sex-typing (woman, good cook; man, executive)? Any stereotyping? Can you detect the influence of TV and ads?

Continue to explore on your own:

1. SEND OUT A QUESTIONNAIRE, or INTERVIEW people you know, young and old. Ask each to list the characteristics of an ideal man and then of an ideal woman, ranked from most important to least important. Help them by beginning, "A man should be . . ." and "A woman should be. . . ."

2. Freely write, nonstop, your impressions from these interviews. What strikes you?

3. CLIP a few ADS from magazines which depict this society's view of the ideal man or woman. Freely WRITE a page debunking what you consider the commonly held (but in your opinion false and stereotyped?) view of men or women today. (You can make a COLLAGE of these pictures to accompany your essay or article.)

4. Now, for fun, picture our society's Ideal He and Ideal She on a date. If you like, sit comfortably, close your eyes for a few moments, and simply let tensions drain down your body and out through your feet. Visualize

66

He and She walking into a fancy restaurant. . . . What is she wearing? Notice facial expressions, posture, gesture, watch them move to a table and sit down. Can you hear them order? What are they saying to each other?

Open your eyes, and write that dialogue. Write freely, nonstop, and exaggerate for fun if it makes your point.

He: "I'm. . . ."
She: "I'm. . . ."

Or, begin by describing America's Ideal Couple.

Here's a sample:

The enormous floor-to-ceiling windows of the Starlight Room were filled with a breath-taking patchwork of runway markers and warning flashers, quiescent now but swept into frenzied motion whenever a plane landed or took off. But Victor had eyes only for Carla. Indeed, he thought to himself as he looked her over appraisingly, she seemed as cool as the martini that languished in her delicate fingers. Her dress of plum velvet, clinging to the delicious globes of her breasts with decadent regality, caressed the curves of her hips also. Her hair, like tiny gold wires (though the conceit was hardly his), tumbled down a finely sculptured head to frame the face, the luminous vacant eyes, the sensually parted lips, in a curly golden aura of femininity.

Only the presence of forty other diners and a *maitre d'* prevented him from leaping across a bowl of bread sticks and two chilled fruit cups to take her then and there. How he longed to crush her against his feverish chest, to press that jello softness until it spread all through him, soothing away the anvil weight of the day. Instead, he ordered for the both of them—*canard à l'orange*—not bothering to ask her preference because he knew it made no difference. She would gladly follow where he led because she was like that.

She, in turn, lowered her eyes in a well-practiced

gesture, suggestive of an innocent gullibility, and tried to transmit by body language her complete submission to his commanding will . . . even though she hated duck.

(James Jenkins)

Rather than satirize "sexual politics," as Jenkins does, write an essay exploring what makes for a healthy relationship. Take off from a quotation you've read that hits the mark, or write freely from one of these:

1.
"Hard as it is for many of us to believe,
women are not really superior to men in
intelligence or humanity—they are only equal."

(Anne Roiphe, 1972)[2]

2.
". . . it is incongruous with the nature of love
to try to reduce the loved person to 'an item
in one's personal world,' or to try to make
him comply with one's demands, or to try to
exert power over him in whatever way."

(Andras Angyal, 1951)[3]

3.
"and the great renewal of the world will
perhaps consist in this, that man and maid,
freed of all false feelings and reluctances,
will seek each other not as opposites, but
as brother and sister, as neighbors, and will
come together *as human beings*. . . ."

(Rainer Maria Rilke, 1903)[4]

[2] Anne Roiphe, "Confessions of a Female Chauvinist Sow," *New York Magazine* (Oct. 1972).
[3] Andras Angyal, "A theoretical model for personality studies," *Journal of Personality*, Vol. 20, Sept. 1951.
[4] Rainer Maria Rilke, *Letters to a Young Poet* (New York, 1963), pp. 38-39.

4.

"Embraces are Cominglings: from the
    Head even to the Feet;
And not a pompous High Priest entering
    by a Secret Place."

(William Blake, 1804)[5]

5.

"In front of every human being, I should support
him, understand him, be free of him and respect his
freedom, and remember what we have in common;
yes, in front of *all* others. But I know I am not capa-
ble. Let me at least try to be like that in front of
you, because you are my friend, because you pre-
pared the way for me and made the task easier for
me. So in your presence at any rate I should not
allow myself any weakness; all our meetings should
be sacred moments."

(René Daumal, 1953)[6]

Did you notice
  —*anything surprising about people's attitudes?*
  —*something new about your own?*
  —*whether we're all influenced by stereotyped thinking?*
   to what degree?

Experiment 21
Freely write your gripe

1. Write across the top of your pad: "WHAT REALLY
   GETS ME MAD?" Turn the page over and write at
   the top: "WHAT CAN WE DO ABOUT IT?"

2. Open with your relaxing exercise (p. 16).

3. Start writing nonstop, talking on paper as fast as you
   can. If more than one thing occurs to you, fine. Write
   your BIGGEST GRIPE(S). Get it all out!

[5] William Blake, "Jerusalem," *The Poetry and Prose of William Blake*, ed.
David Erdman (New York, 1970), p. 221.
[6] René Daumal, *Chaque fois que l'aube paraît* (Paris, 1953). Translated
from the French.

4. When you turn the page, BRAINSTORM on paper, in a list if you like, all the ways to improve the situation. Be funny or serious or both. Try for FIVE SOLUTIONS.

Optional: for practice in convincing your reader:

1. Write two versions of this material:
   a. one which makes your reader respond, "Yes, this writer really believes what she's saying,"

                     and

   b. one which causes your reader to respond "Yes, I believe this, too."

2. TRY OUT your material on a few people, asking them to tell you what part convinces them.

Did you notice
   —*how strong the writing sounds when emotion's involved? where things "heat up"? where you sound really sure?*
   —*you have a sense of humor about your gripes once you write them out? a new perspective?*
   —*how responsive your listeners are to the voice coming through?*
   —*if others feel they share your gripe, and enjoy hearing it expressed so fervently?*

ESPECIALLY FOR BUSINESS AND
FOR LETTER WRITERS

Experiment 22
Send a letter that gets action

What specific things can you do to make people respond favorably to what you say, and take the steps you suggest?

1. WRITE A LETTER that gets someone to do something. First decide what exactly you want the reader of your letter to do.

—Send a refund?
—Vote against a law?
—Take your suggestions for improving business?
—Speak at your group?
—Correct your bill?
—Buy something?
—Advise you?

Or you can write a letter to the editor of a newspaper or magazine in response to an article that stirred up strong feelings in you.

2. VISUALIZE who'll read this letter. Put yourself in her shoes: What would you want, or *not* want, to hear first?

   Write a first sentence that says right out what's the story, but also touches on the interests of or benefits to your reader. Don't beat around the bush. Experiment until you strike just the right note, find just the right tone. Benefits to the reader might be:
   —Getting money or goods
   —Creating good will for her company
   —Keeping a customer
   —"Doing right by" someone
   —Being congratulated (sincerely!)
   —Being praised (sincerely!)
   —Meeting someone interesting
   —Being humanitarian
   —Helping out

3. To write the body of the letter and find the most convincing reasons, find the question your letter could answer, put it at the top of a scratch sheet, and WRITE NONSTOP for five minutes. Sample questions might be:
   —How will it benefit this company to make good on my complaint and pay me $50 for my trouble?
   —How would this restaurant benefit from putting in a nonsmoker's room?
   —How will my reader benefit from what I propose? (If I were in his shoes, what would I want? How can doing what I ask get him that?)

—What good news (praise, money coming) can I provide before I give my criticism or advice? (What are the ways this person can improve her business? How can I put it so she'll listen?)

4. Underline the best reasons, and "talk out" on paper a few lines about each one. Write up as a paragraph.
   —Use *you* more than *I*.
   —Omit any parts in which you sound like a crank or a wiseguy: be sure your tone doesn't put people off (check each sentence).

5. Close with a question, or suggest some small action your reader can take right now (something that's not too much for your reader to do, but gets things moving in the direction you want). Ask for exactly what you want:
   —Could you credit my account with $214.17?
   —How can we improve sales?
   —Can we get together on the fifteenth of June?
   —Could you find out for me who would know? Call me at ——.
   —Won't you report potholes to your town's maintenance department? Call in now.

6. Read your letter to others, and listen for tone. Ask: what's coming through? Locate and omit any sentences which may get a response you don't want. Keep in mind what exactly you want your reader to do.

7. Type your final draft so the letter looks neat on the page, and has no spelling errors. And SEND!

Did you notice
   —*if you hedge, or if you tell what the letter's about in the first sentence or as soon as possible?*
   —*you have a new perspective on your letter if you can put yourself in your reader's shoes?*
   —*you sometimes sound rather formal but you can try a more conversational style that strikes just the right note?*
   —*how important tone of voice is? and how necessary*

it is to hear what's coming through in what you write?
—*any falseness at moments in your letter? or hostility or condescension? that you didn't hear but others did?*
—*if it's useful to write a question with a question mark to encourage a response (as in conversation)? it's important to spell out one small concrete action the reader can take now?*
—*a new style or voice emerging that works well for you? what makes for effective communication?*

For practice, look over the sample letters below.
—Would you do what each letter suggests?
—Does the tone coming through work well?
—How would you improve the letter? Write your version.
Perhaps begin a file of "Model Letters for All Situations."

SOME MODEL LETTERS:

• Inviting a celebrity to speak to your group

LETTERHEAD

Date

Mr. Robert Jones
10 Round Hill Road
Columbus, Ohio ZIP

Dear Mr. Jones,

Would you honor us by addressing our membership at our annual meeting in June? You're our first choice because of your broad knowledge of North American birds. Last year, an exhibit of your lithographs attracted a large audience here. It was the most successful program we ran!

73

We're a non-profit art and nature center unique in this area. We're eager to have you with us. Can you speak here on June 16 at 8 p.m.? Please phone me at 000-000-0000 in any case so we can have a few words together.

Thank you so much.

Very truly yours,

Janet Thomas

Janet Thomas
Program Chairman

• Third notice to get someone to renew membership
  at the local Nature Center

LETTERHEAD

Date

Dear Member,

What would you have missed if you hadn't been a member of the S— Museum and Nature Center this year? The art reception for noted sculptor R— N—; the Wild-flower Walk; the hand-built pottery demonstration; free admission to the Harvest Festival; a night at the Observatory; and reduced fees for all courses.

Your membership not only provided funds for these programs, but also helped us keep 200 acres of natural woodlands for our city. Your support kept us green.

Also, in 19—, the Museum had programs for 30,000 school children, most at no charge. We had an inner-city program, workshops for teachers, and ran special events in local nursing homes. Your support kept these alive.

Please join us again. Our new program promises head-line-making pop art exhibits, unusual craft demonstrations, sheep shearing and maple sugaring, family events for members only, and new art and nature classes. Won't you see the enclosed envelope, and be a member again in 19—?

Yours truly,

Louise Spirer

Louise Spirer
Director

Experiment 23
Persuade with plain English

When you feel there's too much jargon in your writing, and you could be clearer and more to the point, experiment with plain English.

1. GROW A LIST of words that live only in business letters. Find a word or phrase you could say instead. Like this:

Words and Phrases in "Business-ese"	Say instead in plain English[1]
Enclosed please find	Here's, Enclosed is
pursuant to our next meeting	When we next meet
in lieu of	instead of
make inquiry regarding	ask
meets with our approval	we approve
regret to advise	we're sorry
came to my attention	saw
in the event that	if _____
effectuate, deem, transpire,	_____, _____,
inasmuch as, pertaining to,	_____, _____

---

[1] Writing plain English means writing a sentence just as you'd say it out loud.

For instance, you've written, "Fear never came into thought." But would you *say* it like that? You'd probably say, "It never occurred to me to be afraid," or, "I wasn't afraid."

Here's your test for plain English: would you say this sentence if you were talking to someone? If not, how *would* you say it?

2. TAKE A SONG or maxim, and "maximize": put it into business lingo. Use a thesaurus to find long words to substitute for short ones. READ ALOUD to someone: can your listener guess the original?

3. Take a letter, memo, or page from a report, and "make it bad": load it with extra words, legal or business jargon so that you want to say, "What?" when you hear such a long convoluted sentence. Overdo. Use "it is" and "there is" often. Read aloud to someone, and notice her reaction. Is your writing so obviously bad, it's funny?

4. Take that letter, memo, or report, and WRITE IT IN PLAIN ENGLISH, trying to be simple, direct, to the point. When you're stuck, and don't know how to say what you mean, try Experiment 30, p. 143.

5. Read aloud your make-it-bad version and your make-it-better version without telling your listener which is which. Is the difference clear? Do some parts sound the same in both? Do you prefer one version? Why?

Did you notice
—*whether your tone and choice of words suit your meaning? does it sound self-important to use big words when writing about a routine matter?*
—*whether your plain English version has a helpful "let's-work-together-to-get-the-job-done" tone?*
—*your plain English version is clearer? it's a relief to write that way when giving instructions or explanations?*
—*the more you try plain English, the easier it comes when you want it? if you're more persuasive and to the point?*
—*your reader appreciates not having to ferret out your meaning? when you're clear about what you say, she is too?*

LETTERHEAD

Date

TO: THE CONTROLS TASK FORCE

FROM: Darryl Poole

Pursuant to our planned meeting later on this week, we should all review the areas of agreement and findings of the prior meeting held on February 9.

After lengthy discussion we have agreed to some basic needs for definitions as regards RT & Z Controls as referenced during the minutes of the February 9 meeting.

Probably we should reconsider the assignment of control responsibilities as the proper development of guidelines for controls must reside with the most closely associated professional representative of the specific discipline or disciplinary area concerned with delivery and/or administrative responsibility and/or authority. Therefore we should limit our overview level accordingly, and commence by targeting a definition of controls. Our basic position should be to assist and establish a commonality in both vocabulary pertaining to the amount of control we want to develop and the relative means to establish control levels with a high degree of effectiveness and a low degree of problems.

Insofar as we are dealing with a time problem, we should expect a discussion at our next session. The tougher part of the mission will be finding the initial direction which will provide adequate relief for those systems experiencing the aforementioned control problems, and to formulate a relative means to gauge the practical applications of control perspectives. We need to set limits on the range to which we propose extending our somewhat limited resources and keep in mind an overall view of what we plan to accomplish.

* * *

LETTERHEAD

Date

TO: THE CONTROLS TASK FORCE

FROM: DARRYL POOLE

RE:[1] DECIDING ON A DEFINITION OF CONTROLS

Our more important contribution is likely to be establishing a definition of RT&Z Controls others may develop guidelines for.

We all left the meeting on February 9 concerned with these questions:

- How much control do we want to develop?
- How do we develop practical control levels without bogging down?
- How can we develop a common vocabulary for systems controls?

---

[1] Notice how the writer uses "RE." ("regarding") to identify the subject. You can do this in letters, too, before Dear Mr. —. Instead of a lengthy first sentence ("In response to your letter dated January 12, 1980, I'm writing to tell you that we can . . ."), try this:
RE: YOUR REQUEST FOR A REFUND (1-12-80)
Dear Mr. Jones,
I'm sorry we can't send you a check, but we're crediting. . . .

Our efforts should produce three results:

1. short-term relief for systems experiencing control problems,
2. a report on the range of control perspectives,
3. an overall plan for operations integrity.

Again, how much control do we want to develop? We'll plan to spend much of our next session on this question.

SHAPING WHAT COMES

What do you say and how do you say it? No matter how impressive your facts, if you sound like a crank when you present them, you'll lose your reader.

Reading out loud helps you hear what's coming through. Listen to your opening sentence: if you read that, how would you respond? Would you go on?

You want to sound reasonable, fair, intelligent, sincere, straightforward. You don't want to bore, irritate, or confuse. If you were talking with someone, and could see her response as you spoke, you'd know you were going on too long. Are you as effective on paper as you are in person? You can be!

Listen for tone of voice. Consider your reader's interests, and speak to them, if only to keep her reading so you have the chance to make your case.

Here are some patterns for organizing your material:

1. Move from a simple familiar idea to a more complex one. (Choose an example or a comparison from ordinary life that your reader understands.)
2. Go from the most easily proven point (the most readily acceptable) to the least (especially if what you propose is threatening or unusual).
3. Use examples to support your view, moving from least to most convincing. Build a strong case, and clinch it.

To sum up, when you're shaping what comes, try this:

1. Picture your reader and step into her shoes. Now, what would convince you?

2. Write as you speak, in your natural voice. Don't be high-sounding, but reasonable.
3. Develop one aspect in a paragraph, then move on.
4. Are you creating a sense of something building? Save the clincher for last.
5. Try out this writing on others, asking what tone comes through. Any strong reactions to certain parts? Any jargon, or confusing places? (Try Exp. 30).
6. Type up; proofread so it's perfect and looks good.

Have you discovered an approach, a voice or a style that works for you?

With letter, memo, or report in hand, look over the appropriate check list below.

A CHECK LIST FOR LETTER WRITERS

• *What response do I want? What would I need to hear to respond like that?*

• *Just the right tone? Not self-important or condescending? You-centered, positive, courteous? Talking person-to-person for our mutual benefit? (Experiment to find the best tone.)*

Beginning

• *First sentence makes the reader want to continue? Touches on her interests or benefits?*

• *Facts up front right away in plain English? Don't have to wait two paragraphs, or ferret out the meaning?*

• *Good news first? (money coming, what he's been waiting to hear, compliment or thanks when deserved, apology if needed)*

• *If it's bad news, first reassure your cooperation, interest, goodwill?*

Middle

• *"Here are the facts" step by step? Doesn't sound slanted?*

• *Specific examples? Best order?*

- *One sentence, one idea? (Too long? Break in two.) One paragraph, one aspect? (Start a new paragraph?)*

End

- *Ask specifically for what you want?*

- *Try a question with question mark?*

- *Suggest some small thing your reader can do now?*

Revising

- *Need to tighten? Cut out extra words. Do I need this sentence at all? Cut out timeworn jargon—sounds better?*

- *Need to sharpen? Too many "it is" and "there was"? Try active verbs instead (we found, we sent). Would you say it like this over coffee? Confusing? Try plain English.*

- *All the facts your reader needs?*

- *Is it clear?*

- *No typos or misspellings? Check a dictionary.*

A CHECK LIST FOR MEMO AND REPORT WRITERS

- *Who's reading this, and what does he want to know?*

- *Concise, complete, clear?*

- *Purpose plain? Your tone suits it?*

- *Facts right? No omissions or inaccuracies?*

- *Main points covered? Easy to find? Carry conviction? Sequence logical? Paragraphing emphasizes points? Conclusion valid?*

- *Attractive looking? Enough white space? Easy to read? No typos, misspellings? Not monotonous, boring, irritating, confusing? (Tighten and sharpen. Try plain English.)*

81

Beginning

- *A long report? Start with a summary first: what you found, what it means (what's the bottom line?).*

- *Try out a livelier lead (like the first line of a newspaper story).[1] Key facts first, rather than rambling details?*

Middle

- *Paragraphing and headings stress each of your findings? Most useful order for your reader? Progresses logically?*

- *Define terms, supply examples? Use transitions to smooth the way, for easier reading, such as:*
  For example, First, Second, Next, Thus, This means . . . Here's a simple explanation of . . . To make this specific . . .

End

- *Ties in with the beginning?*

- *Your "clincher" comes last?*

- *Leaves a clear final impression? Your reader understands what to do?*

PERSUADING SOMEONE TO HIRE YOU:

AN EXPERIMENT IN WRITING YOUR RESUME

"Write a résumé? But I haven't done anything special." You've got plenty to say: here's how to get going.

1. Open with your relaxing exercise (p. 16).

2. WRITE THREE LISTS, nonstop, headed this way:
   Where I worked, what I did, what they said about me
   Any special responsibilities? What did this job teach you? What were you praised for? Recall your boss's exact words? Learn any special skill?

---

[1] Suggested in Rudolph Flesch, *On Business Communications* (New York, 1972), pp. 129-30.

Where I went to school and what I studied

What degrees did you earn? Any fellowships, awards, special honors? Even if you didn't finish (or are about to), list the school, and what areas of study interest you. Any special projects that showed you abilities you didn't know you had?

What am I good at?

What do people tell you you're good at? Ask! Work well with others? Good organizer? Speak another language? Built your own house? Can program a computer? Write clearly? Inventive?

3. Take a few days to expand these lists. You'll begin to remember things you've done that might demonstrate your drive, ingenuity, skill. Write down everything from high school on. Select later.

4. Underline the most important items, and fill in a first draft of your résumé. Don't simply list items. Use short phrases to describe what you can do, even one or two comments people have made about your work. Make a strong CASE for yourself, without padding. Put highlights in the left margin, so someone can see at a glance the main things you've done.[1]

Try these categories:

NAME

address   phone

<u>EXPERIENCE</u>

highlight   Place of work—most recent goes first. Short phrases tell what you do or have done.

<u>EDUCATION</u>   Place of latest degree. Then earlier schooling.

---

[1] NOTE: Most employers will find this set-up attractive. But if you're sure that the person doing the hiring would prefer an "old-style" résumé, check any manual of résumé writing for models.

PERSONAL   Qualities or interests which might appeal to an employer in this field.

ANNA FUERST
15 Browne St., Lakeville, Mass. 07549   617-555-5555

EXPERIENCE

Publicity
writer

Lakeville Nature Center, Lakeville, Mass., 1979–present

Currently writing press releases announcing programs and giving background information on wide variety of subjects. Write radio copy.

Assistant
public
relations
director

Farmington Community College, Farmington, Mass., 1978–1979

For two years, shared duties of public relations director. Wrote and edited press releases. Complimented on editing ability and "brisk writing style."

Newspaper
columnist

The Lakeville Forum, Lakeville, Mass., 1978–present

Contribute weekly articles on local events. Interview people. Describe coming events.

EDUCATION

English
major

University of Massachusetts, Boston, Mass., 1980

Completing B.A. in English. Work-study experience in journalism.

Lakeville High School, Lakeville,
Mass., 1976

Edited newspaper	Graduated in upper 10%. Edited school paper the year it won a state-wide journalism award.

PERSONAL

Can write on most any subject. Good researcher. Work well with people. Enjoy interviewing. Collect interesting statistics. Play the recorder. Do community volunteer work. Tutor students.

PUBLISHED
MATERIAL

"Digging it," *Massachusetts Magazine*, Oct. '80.

"Tune into Rock to Tune into Youth," *Boston Globe Sunday Magazine*, May '80.

Weekly columns in the *Lakeville Forum*, 1978–present.

Look through the Help Wanted section of the newspaper, and clip ads for jobs that appeal to you. Choose one and, for practice, write your résumé and a cover letter. Send, or place in your folder of "Model Letters."

In the sample cover letter below, notice how the writer highlights one or two qualifications that would be important to the prospective employer.

15 Browne St.
Lakeville, Mass. 07549
Oct. 15, 1980

Mrs. Janice Soames,
Personnel Director
Books-for-Teens Inc.
111 Wayside Drive
Chatham, Mass. 07123

Dear Mrs. Soames,

I'm applying for the job of Writer you advertised in *The New York Times*. I know I can be useful to you in creating stories and articles for teenagers because my present job is much like that: I write all publicity on a wide range of subjects for the local museum.

My experience fits right in with your requirements. The last three years, I've researched and written over 150 articles on such diverse subjects as spring flowers, pop art, spinning and weaving in the colonies, ice harvesting, staining glass. All these were aimed at the non-technical reader.

Enclosed is my résumé. I'll phone you on Monday, Oct. 20. I'd like to come by to show you samples of my writing. Would either Oct. 27 or 29 be convenient? You can phone me at 617-555-5555.

Sincerely,

Anna Fuerst

Anna Fuerst

Should you send out your résumé to agencies or companies listed in the ads you've picked, or is it better for you to call?

Do both. Phone, and ask for the person who's doing the hiring. Establish a personal contact. "I'm _____, and I'm interested in _____. Shall I send my résumé to you?" Your prospective employer might tell you more about the job, and request other information. Put that information in the cover letter (write a separate one tailored to each company); open by mentioning the phone conversation. This way when your résumé arrives, a particular person (whom you've addressed it to) will be waiting to see it. Follow up in a few days with a phone call, and get an interview.

Here's another sample résumé by a woman who returned to school (after eight years) to get a degree in computer science. She complained that she'd "done very little." After trying the experiment, and asking herself questions (about what projects she worked on in graduate school, how she helped students), she came up with several discrete items to list under Experience. And she remembered early interests and accomplishments which, when listed, show off some fine qualities that might catch an employer's attention. Most important, seeing her completed résumé gave her a great boost in confidence!

If you must go two pages, be sure to use most of the second page. Your résumé should be neat, with the most important points striking the eye. For a more professional look, have it typeset.

See Richard Lathrop's *Who's Hiring Who* (Ten Speed Press) for more on this subject.

LUCY DIAMOND
P.O. Box 1234, Easton, Ct. 06812   (203) 742-1007

EXPERIENCE

| Consultant | The Computer Shop, Middlefield, Connecticut, 1978–present |

	Assemble micro systems and instruct users. Starting salary based on $14,000/yr. raised to $20,000/yr.

Assembled
and
programmed
computer

Computer Science Dept., Ohio University, Athens, Ohio
  Put together Challenger II computer, studied its operation, wrote programs in Assembler and Basic. Wrote documentation package, instructed others in its use. Modified an existing Pascal compiler in Basic for it.

College
math
teacher

Math Dept., Ohio University, Athens, Ohio, 1979
  Teaching assistantship. Given evaluations of "excellent" by students. Worked with many foreign students. Praised by dept. chairman for command of subject and ability to teach and tutor well all kinds of students.

Consulted,
wrote
programs

Ohio University, Athens, Ohio, 1978–1979
  Helped graduate students (who were writing dissertations in biology, psychology, etc.) to do the necessary programming.

EDUCATION

M.S.

Ohio University, Athens, Ohio, 1979
  Math and Computer Science. "A" average. Emphasis on data structures, compiler construction, operating systems, numerical analysis. Complimented on writing clear readable programs.

Also attended Ohio State University, Columbus, Ohio, 1978

Studied Assembler, math, man-machine interface. Wrote overview of how the public interacts with computers. Did detailed study of the use of computers by QUBE (two-way cable TV company in Columbus).

A.B.   Barnard College, New York City, N.Y., 1969

Experimental Psychology. Summer Research Assistant. Built electric circuitry system for Skinner box experiment. Prof. Cott said I "worked harder than anybody" he'd ever taught.

Computer programming and mathematics courses, non-credit, summers 1974–1977.

National Science Foundation Summer Science Training Program while in high school. Summers at U. of Oklahoma and Ohio University. First learned to program in 1963.

National Merit Scholar 1965

SPECIAL ABILITIES

Can program in PL/1, COBOL, Pascal, IBM 370 Assembler, FORTRAN.

Persistent and creative in solving problems. Interest in science since childhood. Built, wired, and did plumbing for own house. Fast learner.

Chapter 5
Especially for Students: Writing Papers and Essay Exams

Here are helpful hints nobody may have told you. Writing papers and exams for school won't seem nearly as difficult once you have a format, a way to get going and to shape what comes.

These experiments will help you feel more confident about what to do when you have to write a paper. You'll generate your own thinking about a subject, and end up with a tight paper that makes your point. And you'll feel good about putting together a well-written, thought-provoking piece of writing.

HINTS FOR GETTING BY WHAT STOPS YOU

1. Don't be discouraged by the length of the paper or dissertation. Divide the paper into SECTIONS, and start writing the one you can do right now (try Exp. 28). Write the section you're excited about or know the most about. No need to compose the introduction first—you may want to do that last. Just get going wherever you can, and you'll build momentum.

2. Keep an "Ideas" folder for each section. When something occurs to you, write yourself a note and put it in your collection. This material will stimulate you when it's time to write that part.

3. If you're working on one section and another occurs to you that you need to include, don't get flustered. It's great that you thought of it now. Simply mark the

place the new section belongs (write "Insert A"), head a new page "A" and write a few words to remind yourself what you want to say. Then go on with the section you're writing. Add the new part later.

4. Talk to someone about the place you're stuck, and explain what you have to do. Then write.

5. Work with someone who's also writing a paper and who concentrates well. Being in the room while someone is writing intently may help you do the same.

6. Make a check list of things you still need to do or write for this paper, and put a BIG CHECKMARK next to each item as you complete it. What a satisfying feeling!

7. If something comes up you have to check and you need to speak to someone or go to the library, don't break your momentum. On your CHECK LIST, MAKE A NOTE of what you need to do and the page number you're working on. And KEEP ON with your writing! You can do this other thing later when you need to take a break.

8. Do take a break when you hear yourself say, "I hate this" and "I don't know how to do this part." Leave it. Walk away. Jog. Dance. Come back to it refreshed, or begin on another section.

9. Don't let yourself be overwhelmed: instead of tackling the whole thing, find some small part you can do now, easily. Let the momentum keep you going.

HOW TO ORGANIZE A PAPER QUICKLY

After you've read, made notes, thought, answer this:
• What question do you want your paper to answer? Be *specific*. Write it like you'd say it.

_____

_____

_____?
• How many pages are asked for? _____

Next: *Plan your pages* so you don't spend a lot of time gathering and writing an unwieldy amount of material you won't use (see p. 109).

Example: Your Plan for a Five-Page Paper

p. 1 First paragraph—Introduction
Perhaps open with A PROVOCATIVE QUOTATION that's a take-off point. Use one from the reading you've done or even from a song or poem.
ASK **THE QUESTION,** with a question mark, that this paper will answer.
Second paragraph
Do you need to DEFINE TERMS? Give any more background? Do it here or else
Go on to the **FIRST ASPECT** that needs to be discussed.
You may need more than one paragraph, but keep to ONE PARAGRAPH, ONE ASPECT.
Support main statements with a quotation from one of your sources. MAKE YOUR CASE.
p. 2 **SECOND ASPECT** (go on to the next page if necessary)
p. 3 **THIRD ASPECT**   (")
p. 4 **FOURTH ASPECT**   (")
p. 5 Last paragraph—Conclusion
Re-read your first paragraph. ANSWER the question: so, what's the bottom line on all this?

As you write the paper, check your plan. If you see you're already on page 3 and you've only given background material, you know it's time to answer the question (or reword it!). If you don't have enough pages to go into all the aspects, you could touch on most of them briefly, then say, "but the main one is . . . ," and write the paper largely on that one.

Go into more detail, or include more aspects, if the paper is to be ten pages. But PLAN YOUR PAGES in any case, and check your plan as you write. It'll keep you from going off the track or writing forty pages and then trying to pare them down to four.

TRY THIS TO ORGANIZE A PAPER

Introduction—*Opening quotation.*
             Question you'll answer.
             Define terms?
Body   —*First aspect.*
             Second aspect (new paragraph).
             Third aspect (new paragraph . . . or more).
Conclusion —*Sum up, tie in to opening.*
             Answer your question.

An Example: Your Planning Sheet

Sociology assignment: Five pages on the double standard

p. 1 Quote from Greer—sets the stage
So, *is there a double standard today?*
What does "double-standard" mean? Define briefly.

1–2 First aspect: *biological* data about alleged sex differences (quote studies).

2–3 Second aspect: impact of *family* and *education* on the growing child (quote Roiphe, Millet, Gagnon).

3–4 Third aspect: impact of *society*, values, stereotypes of ideal man and woman (examples from ads, TV).

5 Tie-in to opening:
   Yes, there is a double standard *but* it's changing in these ways: ....

Another Example: Your Planning Sheet

History assignment: Six–ten pages on Frederick the Great, the characteristics of his lifetime that caused him to create a strong German state

p. 1 First paragraph—**Introduction**
      Historians agree (quote one: Johnson? Marriott?) there were several reasons F the G created a strong German state. List the main ones (1–3). *Which of these were most important in his turning Germany into a major European power?* (the question this paper will answer)

p. 2–3 Second paragraph—**1st reason**
        The times, situation in Europe; support major statements with quotations (footnote)

Next paragraph—**2nd reason**
"*His inheritance*," F's father, upbringing, abuse, values, suspicions, desire to pull country together, impact of Enlightenment; influences on the growing boy (quote and footnote)

p. 4 Next paragraph—**3rd reason**
or so His personality, *desire for power*; evidence of this (quote and footnote)

AT THIS POINT, you should be no more than midway in the paper, around page 4.

You've given the background that led to certain events. So, OF THESE FACTORS, WHICH WERE MOST IMPORTANT? What do you think? Was it one thing, or a combination of things, that led to F's greatness?

p. 5   **TRANSITION**—Emergence of (1) F's military
genius and (2) intelligence as an administrator led
to F's success

Next paragraphs—**1st major factor**—*military genius*
Aspects of military genius might include what
F did to make Germany strong: tactics, battles,
upset Austrian supremacy, attack on Silesia,
training small groups, conscription, element of
surprise, ambition, desire for power, "inheritance" from father, etc. (Put these in order,
document with examples, footnote)

p. 6   Next—**2nd factor**—*intelligence as an administra-*
or so   *tor*
Aspects might include: setting up absolute control, centralizing and changing government,
knew value of middle class (commerce, mer-
chants), smart about grain, made profit, coffers
full, etc. (Put these in order, document, footnote)

p. 7   Last paragraph—**Conclusion**—Tie-in with open-
or 8   ing question
Thus, given the times, F the G's military genius and intelligence as an administrator were
major factors in the creation of a powerful German state.

Once you've planned your pages this way, you'll know
where to insert material, where it fits in the "story" you're
telling, where it best helps you make your case.

As you write, check this planning sheet to see where
you are: have you written too much about one aspect,
leaving little space for another? Have you emphasized the
most important points by saying enough about them, and
supported major statements with appropriate quoted material?

Don't worry if you haven't mentioned everything you
know about the subject: your aim is to make a specific

96

point. Does the paper flow from one idea to the next? Is every sentence clear? (See section on Becoming Your Own Best Editor, p. 129 ff.)

WRITING A SCIENTIFIC OR TECHNICAL REPORT
OR DISSERTATION

Experiment 24
Divide the report into sections;
use "There is" instead of "I think"

You've read the literature, run your experiments, and you're ready to tell what you've found.

1. DIVIDE your report INTO SECTIONS. MAKE UP A QUESTION you could answer for each section, such as:

(Title)	WHAT DID I FIND, AND WHAT
Abstract[1] →	DOES IT MEAN?
	(Briefly, your major findings with just enough explanation of what was done so they have meaning)
Introduction →	WHAT'S BEEN DONE OR SHOWN ABOUT THIS ALREADY?
	(Surveying the literature, defining a principle, or giving your hypothesis)
Materials →	WHAT DID I USE IN MY EXPERI-
and Methods	MENT, AND WHAT DID I DO FIRST, SECOND, NEXT?
Results →	WHAT HAPPENED? (or) WHAT'S THE STORY ABOUT THIS PHENOM- ENON?
	(Just the facts; what do your graphs and tables show?)
Discussion →	WHAT DO THE RESULTS MEAN?
	(Interpret your findings in light of other research)

---

[1] To write an abstract, see p. 99.

Conclusion→   IN A NUTSHELL, WHAT HAVE I SHOWN? IMPLICATIONS OR FUTURE DIRECTIONS? (Your conclusions?)

2. Choose the question you feel you can write about now, and freely talk out the answer on paper.

3. You're in motion now: try doing another section the same way. Take a break when you need it: walk around, stretch, have an apple, relax face and limbs. Then try the question, writing nonstop.

4. When you have a rough draft of all sections, and any tables or charts you want, write your first draft, in logical order, beginning to end.

   To take on the scientific or impersonal tone of voice appropriate to this kind of report, SUBSTITUTE "there is," "one sees," and "we find" wherever you write "I think."

   Or take "I" out by turning the sentence around like this:

Instead of	*Write*
• I put the rats on a schedule of	→ The rats were placed on
• I cut the crystal into	→ The crystal was cut

   OR: substitute "one" for "I"

• I think that	→ One sees that
• It is my opinion that	→ There is

5. If describing a PROCESS, check to see whether you've told the whole story, not omitting any important step. Move through each stage, show its function and its relationship to the whole. Have you found a clear illustration everyone can understand to explain the PRINCIPLE involved here?

6. TRY OUT your first draft on someone outside your field. Ask her to stop you whenever she hears something confusing: where does she get lost?

Did you notice
- *—if you've made something clearer to yourself and your reader?*
- *—if your facts arrive one by one?*
- *—if a reader can follow (and duplicate) what you've done?*
- *—where you need to use plain English to explain something more clearly?*

WRITING AN ABSTRACT OR SUMMARY

Your dissertation requires an abstract of 600 words. Use the same approach as in Experiment 24 to get words on paper, and then try a first draft.

Head a sheet of paper with each of the questions below, and WRITE NONSTOP, "talking" on paper:

I. WHAT DID I DO?
II. HOW DID I DO IT?
III. WHAT DID I FIND?

Use the impersonal tone when you do your first draft. Construct sentences to avoid using *I*. Present your findings as facts: an objective report that sums up what you discovered.

WRITING ABOUT LITERATURE

Experiment 25
Immerse yourself, discover your slant

1. CHOOSE a writer or work you really enjoy and want to spend time with.

2. READ as much as possible, especially when you want fresh food for thought. Immerse yourself in this writer's novels, stories, poems.

3. COLLECT IN YOUR NOTEBOOK striking passages or quotations.[2] If lengthy, write the opening

---

[2] This step was suggested by Dr. Yakira Frank (U. of Ct.)

line, and a note about the rest. Be sure to write down book and page number. Look for:

—recurring *themes* or ideas, and changes in themes
—repeated *images* and *words* (*live, wake, wind, birch*)
—*striking lines* (vivid, well-said, moving)
—favorite *stylistic devices* and *variations in techniques* (from earlier to later works)
(Does this author ask rhetorical questions? Coin words? Use slant rhymes? Vary length of sentences? Use sensory specifics or abstract terms?)

4. READ LETTERS and essays about writing, by your writer.

How does this person see the creative process? the aim of a writer? Write down striking quotations, book, and page number.

5. Start a "THEY SAY" folder or section in your notebook. Look up your writer in the card catalogue at the library, and find out what others say about her work. Or search through critical editions and anthologies of essays about her (bookstores carry these). Jot down any statement that strikes you, and note author, title, city of publication, year, and page number.

6. DISCOVER YOUR SLANT. First, read through your notes and underline highlights. Set aside. Write across the top of a blank sheet: "What strikes me about this author's writing?"

7. Do your basic relaxing exercise (p. 16).

8. Pick up the sheet, and write nonstop by "talking out" whatever occurs to you. Keep the pen moving. Begin anew with any sentence. Cover two pages if you can.

9. You're in motion now. Read over, underline highlights, and see if you can ASK YOURSELF THE QUESTION YOU WANT TO ANSWER about this person's work. Place that question on the top of another sheet. Ask something such as:

100

—What's the best part of this writer's work?
—How are her early writings like (or unlike) her later ones?
—What themes recur? What images?
—What techniques of style stand out?
—What is this writer trying for? Does she succeed?
—What's man's purpose according to this writer?
—What impact has this author had on other writers?
—How is writer A like (or unlike) writer B?

10. Put the question aside for a moment just to take a few breaths in . . . and out. . . . When you're ready, pick up the pad (or sit at the typewriter) and WRITE QUICKLY by "talking out" the answer. Go! (If you want to take it further see Experiments 28–29.)

Did you notice
—*what attracted you to this writer? has that changed?*
—*if reading what others say about her helped you appreciate the writer's work, or made you feel you missed something? did it make you want to read more or not? did you believe these critics just because they're in print, or because they wrote convincing well-documented essays?*
—*you became interested in your writer's life, and how it fed her work?*
—*if you share her view of the world?*

SHAPING WHAT COMES

BEGINNINGS

You know what aspect of a writer's work you'll explore, and you've discovered your slant. You want to show a progression in ideas or techniques from earlier to later works. Or you want to trace one theme. Whatever your focus, let your reader know right away what your paper's about.

To open: Find a provocative or representative quotation, from the writer's work or from a critic's commentary, which serves as a good take-off point. From there, you can elaborate, illustrate, agree or disagree.

Or, try this: ask your reader the question you're going to answer in this paper. A question helps your reader to focus, and makes her want to read on.

As you write your opening and the paper, you might want to follow the conventions for writing about literature (as you did in Exp. 24, putting together a scientific report). For example:

1. Write "we find" and "one sees" instead of "I think" and "my impression is." Use the impersonal tone of voice.
2. When quoting the writer's work or a critic's comments as they appear in print, USE THE PRESENT TENSE (McKay *calls* Thoreau "the philosopher of environment").

About Setting Up Quotations, and Footnoting

When you quote a few lines, use quotation marks around the exact words of someone else. When you quote a long passage, omit the quotation marks, but place the whole passage, single-spaced, in a block, ten spaces from the left margin (see the quote on p. 104). Be sure to footnote direct quotations *and ideas* you've taken from others. Footnotes go at the bottom of the page, or as a list of "Notes" at the end of the paper.

Some Sample Openings

Wordsworth's critics comment on "a great falling off in genius" in later years.[1] Does Wordsworth's earlier poetry surpass his later work? By what criteria can we contrast the two?

* * *

Nowhere do we find such a complete summary of Walt Whitman's thought than in "Democratic Vistas." According to Whitman, what are the needs, what is the promise of this grand experiment America?

* * *

"My study is man," says Nathaniel Hawthorne.[2] What are the assumptions about man that underlie Hawthorne's tales?

* * *

One can approach Emerson's essays "The American Scholar" and "Montaigne; or, The Skeptic" as earlier and later versions of his thought about mankind. What has happened to man that he must be either parrot or skeptic? And what is the remedy?

* * *

Ezra Pound says of Walt Whitman, "He *is* America . . . his time and his people."[3] How did Whitman "celebrate himself" as a new kind of man in this new land?

Some Sample Footnotes

Model:
First and last name of person quoted, "chapter or article," *Book Title* (City of publication, year), p. —.

[1] Lionel Trilling, "The Immortality Ode," *English Romantic Poets*, ed. by M. H. Abrams (New York, 1960), p. 141.

[2] Quoted in F. O. Matthiessen, *American Renaissance* (New York, 1941), p. 225.

[3] Ezra Pound, "What I Feel About Walt Whitman," *Whitman*, ed. by Roy Harvey Pearce (Englewood-Cliffs, N.J., 1962), p. 8.

NOTE: For more on footnotes, and on bibliography, see the *MLA Style Sheet* or the *MLA Handbook* (order from the Modern Language Association, 62 Fifth Ave., N.Y.C., N.Y. 10011).

What you say in your opening paragraph should lead naturally into the rest of your paper. If you're not sure how to organize your material, try one of the patterns suggested below.

Plan A: Technique discovers theme

Look over your material, and underline or put checkmarks next to striking examples of this writer's techniques and themes.

When you consider the themes, what main ideas emerge and recur? Some view of man and his condition? A statement about how we live? List prominent themes; note important passages.

What about techniques? Look closely at the way this writer uses words, phrases, and sentences. How does she build momentum, begin and end sentences? Do you notice that certain words or images are repeated? Does she use jargon, formal words, slang, or plain English? To what effect? Does the writer use mostly sensory specifics or abstract language? Short sentences or long? Note when and where.

What techniques are used when a theme is being brought out strongly? Do long flowing sentences accompany passages which express certain themes? In poetry, does the sound of the line echo the sense of it? Does a line about bees buzz?

Identify prominent characteristics of this writer's style, and discuss them, giving examples from his work. Tie in *how* he says things with *what* he says.

For example, you're writing about Emerson's exploration of "what man can know." You might expect the author to pose abstract questions or write like a philosopher. But you find a striking passage in "The American Scholar" which uses concrete sensory specifics, and you point out Emerson's choice of words:

> What would we really know the meaning of?
> The meal in the firkin; the milk in the pan;

the ballad in the street; the news of the boat;
the glance of the eyes, the form and gait of
the body. . . .[1]

Emerson brings the question back to one's experience here, in this body now in this place. His meaning is mirrored in his level of diction, his choice of words, these sensory specific examples.

Plan B: They Say/I Say

"Statement of the question, negative solution, positive solution"—a strong way to make your case.

In the opening paragraph, ask the question your paper will answer. Be sure to end with a question mark.

In the next paragraph(s), give what others have said about this question, as a background and framework for what you'll say later. What issues about this writer and her techniques does this question raise? Be sure to footnote any direct or re-worded passages from critics.

Write a brief transition, a bridge from what "they say" to what "I say"—but don't use *I*. You're going to tell what you think about all this, but use the impersonal "one sees" and "we find."

For the main part of your paper, give your slant, point by point, so the reader gets a sense of something building. Support with quotations (footnoted) from your writer's work (your "primary" source).

We see that Thoreau . . .

One notes the way in which Whitman . . .

Faulkner himself describes the way he writes in . . .

The speaker[2] of the poem begins by naming . . .

Plan C: Chart out your comparison/contrast

Decide what you'll compare or contrast, and follow the steps described in the following example.

[1] Ralph Waldo Emerson, "The American Scholar," *Selections from Ralph Waldo Emerson*, ed. by Stephen E. Whicher (Cambridge, Mass., 1957), p. 78.
[2] It's conventional to refer to "the speaker" of a poem rather than giving the poet's name, so you preserve the distinction between the poet and the voice she's chosen to use in this one particular poem.

You've planned to show similarities and differences in a writer's earlier and later work. So you've chosen three characteristics of her poetry that will help you make a point about a change in the quality of her perception and expression. You'll discuss these items:

(1) recurrent images
(2) use of rhyme
(3) meter

Try this for a balanced presentation of your material:

1st paragraph of Middle:
    Discuss item 1
    in earlier work.

4th paragraph:
    Discuss item 2
    in later work.

↓   ↓

2nd paragraph:
    Discuss item 1
    in later work.

5th paragraph:
    Discuss item 3
    in earlier work.

↓   ↓

3rd paragraph:
    Discuss item 2
    in earlier work.

6th paragraph:
    Discuss item 3
    in later work.

In each paragraph:
—Quote examples from the text itself (cite source, page.)
—Begin with a "transitional" word or phrase, such as "Similarly" or "In the same way" when you're emphasizing how two things are similar, or use "In contrast" and "Unlike . . ." when you're stressing differences.
—Don't use, "I think." Write, "We find," or, "one sees."

Here's another way you can organize the body of your paper[3]:

---

[3] For more on writing comparisons and contrasts, see pages 62 and 108-113.

1st paragraph of Middle:
    ↓ Discuss earlier work, item 1.
2nd paragraph:
    ↓ Discuss earlier work, item 2.
3rd paragraph:
       Discuss earlier work, item 3.
4th paragraph begins with: "Looking at her later work, we find. . . ." (your transition)
        ↓ 4th paragraph:
           Discuss later work, item 1.
        5th paragraph:
        ↓ Discuss later work, Item 2.
        6th paragraph:
           Discuss later work, item 3.

ENDINGS

Read your beginning so you write an ending that ties in.

Let your reader know that you're concluding: "Thus, we see that . . ."

Try any of these ways to end:

1. AGAIN ASK YOUR QUESTION (in slightly different words?), and give a succinct answer.
2. Sum up your main points.
3. Offer a clincher (one final piece of evidence).

For a thought-provoking final sentence (that sends out ripples in your reader's mind), perhaps:

4. Use one last quotation from your writer that seems to sum it all up for you.
5. Briefly suggest a further line of exploration, the next question.
6. Briefly point out the wider significance of your ideas.

Have you left your reader with a strong single impression?

TITLES

This is a good time to look at the title for your paper. Does it say what your paper's really about?

Your title should be more than the name of the writer and work. Be specific so your reader knows what particular aspect of this author's work you'll discuss:

Blake's Cosmic Sense: "Auguries of Innocence"

William Wordsworth's Lyrics: The Poetry of Wise Passiveness

Walt Whitman, Myth Maker

WRITING ABOUT PEOPLE, ERAS, OR IDEAS

Experiment 26
Plan your pages—choose three bases
of comparison/contrast

This approach will help you economize your time.

1. Decide what two people, eras, movements, or philosophies you'll compare or contrast. X and Y.

2. Read over your notes from class and books, then put aside. Do your relaxing exercise (p. 16).

3. WRITE FIVE QUESTIONS you could explore, on the model of:
   —HOW IS X LIKE Y?
   —HOW WAS X UNLIKE Y?
   —WHAT'S WORTH FINDING OUT ABOUT X AND Y?

4. Narrow your subject as much as you can. For instance, MAKE A LIST OF ITEMS (qualities or characteristics) you might explore.
   Here's a sample:
   You're going to compare/contrast Julius Caesar and Mark Antony.
   You could look at each one's:
   impact on history   ← YOUR
   moral values   LIST
   goals in life
   career as statesman
   relationship with women

108

religious views
military skills

Or, You want to discuss the *Book of Job* and also
Ecclesiastes.

You could look at each one's:
structure
themes   ← YOUR
                                          LIST
    (man's relationship to God,
    man's relationship to man)
impact
way of concluding

5. Choose three items as your "bases" of comparison or
contrast. Choose the points that interest you most.
(You can discuss other items as well if you're asked
to write a longer paper.)

6. Before writing, PLAN YOUR PAGES.[1]
Get an overview of what you need to do, according
to how many pages you've been asked to write.
Here's a sample plan:

Length of paper: 8 pages plus bibliography
Beginning: ½ page
Middle: about 6 pages
End: 1 page

Then ask yourself: In six pages (the body of the
paper), how many items of comparison/contrast
could I cover well?

For example, compare X and Y in terms of items 1,
2, 3 ("compare Emerson and Thoreau in terms of
lifestyles, views of man's possibilities, impact on his
times").

Figure: 1 page on each item, about X, equals 3
pages.
1 page on each item, about Y, equals 3
pages.
Total for Middle: 6 pages

---

[1] Note: You can do this whether or not you're writing a comparison/
contrast. If you're simply explaining "three theories of deviant behavior,"
for example, decide how much space you should allot for each. Then you
won't go on too long and have to discard extra material.

If you know in advance you have only about six pages for the body of your paper, and exactly what you'll write about on each (for a balanced comparison), you'll know what kind of and how much material to get from books.

But be open: perhaps after you research your subject, you may want to discuss only one item in depth.

7. Find the books that seem most helpful, and look up key words (X, Y, the items) in the index. Read the appropriate pages, make notes, jot down striking quotations, plus author, book title, city of publication, year, and page number.

8. To begin writing the paper, ASK YOURSELF a question about each item. WRITE it across the top of a sheet, like this:

Are X and Y basically similar or different in _____ (your item 1)?

YOU
WRITE→ Are the *Book of Job* and *Ecclesiastes* basically similar or different in structure?

Set up three sheets headed this way, one for each item.

9. Put aside these sheets, and sit comfortably for a few minutes. Allow your face and limbs to relax. Then answer the question about item 1: WRITE NON-STOP. Talk out your answers, make note of any passages that occur to you as support for what you're saying.

10. Repeat for each item (relax, look at the question, answer freely nonstop).

11. On another sheet, sum up your slant: write your opener for the body of your paper. Mention all three items, and the overall similarity or difference between the two main things (X and Y) which you'll discuss.

If you're stressing similarity, phrase your opener like this:

YOU → Although the *Book of Job* and *Ecclesiastes*
WRITE differ in structure, they share certain themes, and end in the same way.

If you're stressing differences, you might write:

YOU → The *Book of Job* and *Ecclesiastes* have cer-
WRITE tain themes in common; however, they differ greatly in structure and in the way they end.

12. Put together a first draft: use your opener (step 11) and your discussions of each item (steps 9–10) following the order suggested in your opener. Supplement with quotations to support what you say, and footnote. OMIT sentences that don't contribute to the point you're making.

Begin a new paragraph for each idea you discuss.

SHAPING WHAT COMES

For a balanced comparison, you want to stick to just those bases of comparison (items 1, 2, 3) you chose, and give equal space to each.

Here are the two plans for arranging a comparison or contrast of X and Y. Either you write about X first, discussing each item in a separate paragraph, and then do the same for Y. Or you might take item 1, write one paragraph about X, one about Y, and go on to item 2 and 3 in the same way. Like this:

X—the idea, person, era, book you're comparing to
Y—the other idea, person, era, book
1, 2, 3—your three (or more) bases of comparison (items to be discussed about X and Y)

Organize horizontally: →

1st paragraph:	X 1	then 2nd paragraph:	Y 1
3rd paragraph:	X 2	then 4th paragraph:	Y 2
5th paragraph:	X 3	then 6th paragraph:	Y 3

Or, Organize vertically ↓

1st paragraph: X 1
2nd paragraph: X 2
3rd paragraph: X 3

Transition ("In contrast" or "Similarly")

4th paragraph: Y 1
5th paragraph: Y 2
6th paragraph: Y 3

Of course, it may take more than a paragraph to discuss item 1 about X ("Julius Caesar's goals"); just be sure to give equal time to item 1 about Y ("Mark Antony's goals").

A CHECK LIST FOR PAPER WRITERS

—*Does the opening sentence give my subject and my slant, and lead into the items discussed next?*

—*Do I support my statements with specifics, such as quoted material? Two examples at least for each point I make?*

—*Do I stick to "one paragraph, one aspect," and not go off on a tangent? Any sentences that don't belong or should be moved?*

—*Do I stick to the bases of comparison I chose, giving "equal time" to each side of the comparison/contrast?*

—*Do I use enough "TRANSITIONS" to begin paragraphs and prepare my reader for a shift in ideas?*

Here are some useful words to begin paragraphs and signal what you're doing.

When your're COMPARING what just came with what's coming:	When you're CONTRASTING what just came with what's coming:
Too,	In contrast,
Similarly,	However,
Likewise,	Unlike
In the same way,	On the other hand,
... share ...	... differ ...
... have in common ...	... do not share ...

When you're CONCLUDING,
tying in what just came
with your final words:

Thus,
Therefore,
So we see,
In conclusion,
To sum up,
Finally....

See pages 136–137 for a list of more transitions you can use.

See page 107 about endings and titles for this paper.

WRITING ESSAY EXAMS

Experiment 27
Take five minutes to write this scratch sheet

If it's exam time there's no need to panic. Practice writing a scratch sheet, and you'll have a way to get down your thoughts without wasting a moment.

1. Read the question carefully. Circle key words.

2. Write a scratch sheet you'll follow. Check your watch —spend *only five* minutes, and start writing the essay.

FILL-IN:

What's asked *for?*   *(Re-phrase in your own words AS A QUESTION.)*

Key term *to define?*   *(If there is, write a phrase defining it.)*

What do **I think?**   *(Yes, no, yes but . . . note your main view.)*

Because
  reason #1
  example (e.g.)
              (Jot down main reasons, and any examples of support or an appropriate quotation.)

  reason #2
  example
              (Don't dwell: if you can't think of an example right away, start writing the essay anyway.)

CHECK your watch: time to write!

3. Start writing the essay like this:
Paragraph 1: Re-state the question in your words.
          2: (if appropriate) Key term and how you mean it.
          3: Your answer ("I think . . . because . . . ") and your reasons. Elaborate. Support with examples.
          4: Next reason, examples ("Also, . . . ").
          5: Next reason, examples (Moreover, . . .").
          6: Sum up. Tie in with opening question ("Thus").

Here's a sample. Your exam reads:
"Was Jesus a revolutionary? Was Paul? Discuss."

You immediately fill out a scratch sheet:

Question: Was Jesus a rev.? Was Paul?
Key term: "revolutionary" meaning "one who . . ."
I think: Jesus, yes, Paul, no

Because:	• What J. did	Then do	• just followed
First	at . . .	Paul:	e.g. verse #
do	e.g. verse #	no he	• didn't . . .
Jesus:	• also what he	wasn't	e.g. as in . . .
yes he	did at . . .		• ?
was	• e.g. cited in . . .		e.g. ?
	His teachings		
	e.g. such as in		
	sermon . . .		
	and . . .		

Five minutes are up.
    Start writing.
        Keep going:
        get down on paper as much as you can.

Did you notice
    —if you shaped the answer right away, rather than los-
    ing time in a panic, or writing haphazardly?
    —if your essay moves well, building your case?

PART 3

FINDING YOUR WAY
FROM NOTES TO
FIRST DRAFT

There are many ways to get moving so you can immediately write whatever you want.

If you have *no idea* what to write about, see "How to Find What You Want to Write" (below).

If you have a *subject*, and want to narrow it, and start writing, see "Suppose I Have a Subject—Now What?" (p. 120).

If you already have a specific *question* you want to answer, turn to Experiment 28, page 122.

HOW TO FIND WHAT YOU WANT TO WRITE

WRITE across the top of a page: "What would I like to write about?" Do your relaxing exercise (p. 16). "TALK on paper"[1] nonstop for a page. Do this again at another time. Underline highlights: Do you see anything worth developing?

Or, let your environment and your own writing stimulate you. Follow through on an item or two from the lists below. Then write nonstop for ten minutes about any idea that's occurred to you.

WHERE TO LOOK	WHAT TO TRY
your "ideas" folder (see p. 6)	eavesdrop
diary	observe people in pressure situations
journal	observe people in social situations
dreams you wrote down	
newspaper headlines	interview people

---

[1] Rudolph Flesch and others use the phrase "talk on paper" to mean write as you speak, in plain English. I mean it to imply that you can write as *easily* as you talk. To "talk on paper," here, means free-flow nonstop.

WHERE TO LOOK	*WHAT TO TRY*
your "Clippings" folder (p. 7)	take a survey on a burning question
advice-to-lovelorn column	record a conversation
bathroom walls	record a fight
bars, parties	imagine the best thing that could happen now
hobbies	pretend you're a . . .
gravestones	imagine a modern hero or heroine
family photos	re-do a dream's ending
other writers	watch the wind in the trees
myths	imagine What If . . . ?
the Bible	talk about what's worth knowing
history books	make up a writing experiment
maps	go somewhere new, and notice!
paintings	
your ethnic background	
the landscape	

"SUPPOSE I HAVE A SUBJECT—NOW WHAT?"

You're going to narrow the subject, so focus in on just what aspect you'll write about.

If the task seems too big, agree that for now you'll do only the ten-minute writing suggested below, simply as a warm-up, for the sheer good feeling of putting words on paper. You don't have to plan what you'll write. In just ten minutes, you'll discover how to start painlessly, and how to build momentum.

Write your subject in CAPITAL LETTERS across the top of a page, and leave it.

If you're the least bit anxious about writing, and feel that you have too much or not enough to say, make room for a fresh impulse. Take two minutes to "un-clutch." Turn from listening to your thoughts to relaxing your body, and trust that everything you want to express will come without strain. Right now,

Open with your relaxing exercise (p. 16).

Start Anywhere, Keep Talking on Paper	When you open your eyes, read what's on the page and simply start anywhere. Double space. Pretend you're telling a story to a friend. Talk it
Double Space	out. Don't worry about paragraphs, awkward places, spelling: just keep
Keep Going!	going! You'll shape it later. Talk about the subject or (to keep the pen or carriage moving) about your sense impressions now. Don't grope for the right word: keep writing. Good!

Try for two pages, and stop.

Notice that when writing this way you're never stuck. You don't start from any particular point, but can *begin anew with any sentence.* You can always describe your sensory impressions—fingers tapping the keys, your feet on the floor, the sound of the wind—and write that just to keep words coming out.

Now you're in motion. Time to focus in.

UNDERLINE anything that strikes you, that hits the mark.

FIND A QUESTION in these highlights. Be specific. Ask yourself what, how, or why . . . ?

Perhaps you want to describe your pet project. Ask yourself: What's this project about, and who'll benefit?

Do you want to convince your favorite restaurant's manager to separate smokers and non-smokers? Ask: How would it help business to have a non-smokers' room?

Whatever you want to write—an essay, report, proposal, or letter—get busy by finding a question you can answer.

Try Experiment 28.

Experiment 28
Ask your question,[2] answer freely

To warm up, see pages 120–121.

1. Write or type your question, with question mark, across the top of the page, and leave it.

2. Relax from head to toe.

3. WRITE NONSTOP whatever comes to you. Trust that answers will appear once you're in motion. "Talk" on paper. Start anew with any sentence. Keep going.

4. After two pages, read over what you've written, and underline highlights, anything that "hits the mark."

5. You've got momentum. Repeat Experiment 28 with another question, more specific than the first.

6. When you have a lot of material, go on to Experiment 29.

Did you notice
—*a few surprisingly well-turned phrases?*
—*that things are bubbling up in you now?*
—*you've managed to get some good ideas into words on paper?*
—*you've found a painless way to get going, to push your own start button?*

You've tried Experiment 28, and you have pages with underlinings, and perhaps some notes as well. "This must be where the hard part comes in," you'll probably say.

But getting going and generating ideas is the hard part and now something's about to take shape!

When you write the first draft, remember you're not trying to show off how much you can put into it; you're

[2] Such as: "What can I do that they'd want to hear about?" "How can we sell more shoes?" "Have women been discriminated against throughout history?" "What's this project about, and who'll benefit?"

more interested in being true to your vision of things, and being clear.

Let Experiment 29 help you produce a working draft of the whole piece.

Experiment 29
Talk in paragraphs: What's the story?

Arrange Highlights on a "Main Points" Sheet

1. Read over underlinings and notes. Arrange highlights as a list of main points, numbering according to what you should say first, next, last. If the order isn't clear to you yet, do you see a NATURAL STARTING POINT? Begin there for now.

"So What's It All About?"

2. Imagine talking with a friend who asks, "So what's it all about?" Begin at the beginning, and "tell" her straight out. "Talk" in paragraphs. Double space this.

"Talk" in Paragraphs

3. Begin a new paragraph each time you shift gears, bringing in a new idea, or intensifying what you said last. Paragraphs can be short. You can leave space on the page if you haven't got all the facts to feed in yet.

One Paragraph, One Aspect

The point is to keep going. Stick to "one paragraph, one aspect."

"And So?"

Each paragraph moves the piece forward. When there's a lull (you're not sure where to go next), it's as if your friend asks, "And so?"

New Paragraph

New paragraph. "Talk" out on paper everything you can.

Keep Going!

Feed in All Your Highlights

4. Spread pages with underlinings around you so they catch your eye, and can feed your writing. Later, you'll tighten, sharpen, re-arrange,

123

correct. Now, just concentrate on developing as many ideas as you can, and getting them down on paper.

Briefly List Points You'll Get to

5. If, as you're writing, a flurry of points you want to cover occurs to you, take only a minute to jot them down on your "main points sheet." Then get back to the idea you're developing.

Keep on "Talking" in Paragraphs

When you run out of steam for a moment, look to your "main points sheet," and take up the next item that logically follows from the one you just wrote. "Talk" in paragraphs about the next main point you feel you can write about now.

Feed in from All Your Sources

6. And you need to check something (find a quotation, a statistic or a book), go ahead. Your essay is building now: this is your first draft, so feed in as much as you can.

Check Your Main Points Sheet

7. What do you need to say next? Check off each point on your list. Have you covered everything?

Read Your Opening Tie In, Sum Up

8. Read your opening. You want your final words to tie-in. Can you sum up in a sentence or two what this piece is about?

* * *

Congratulations! You've come a long way from that blank sheet of paper.

Cut Up, Rearrange

If you want to work a little more on this draft, look for sentences and paragraphs that obviously fit better in an earlier or later place. Don't bother re-typing now. Just cut up and rearrange, as if you were fitting together

124

the pieces of a puzzle. Tape the parts into the order that's easiest to follow.

Let it Rest
if You're Tired

Important: If you're tired, let it rest for now. You'll see "what-fits-where" much more clearly when you take a fresh look later.

Did you notice
—momentum helps you write? that it's useful to start writing rather than thinking about it?
—you had more to say than you thought before you started?
—that writing about one idea stimulated other ideas?

To sum up:

SEVEN STEPS TO HELP YOU WRITE

1. *Write a question you want to answer*
2. *Relax from head to toe*
3. *"Talk" nonstop on paper*
4. *Underline highlights*
5. *Arrange a main points list*
6. *"Talk" in paragraphs: what's the story*
7. *Rest, then revise*

GIVE YOURSELF AN ENCOURAGING WORD

Whenever you're pleased by what you wrote, like now when you have a first draft, take a minute at the height of your enthusiasm to make yourself a sign or note expressing how you feel. Look at it when you doubt what you've done is any good. We all need an encouraging word.

TWELVE THINGS TO TRY WHEN YOU'RE STUCK

You're in the middle of writing something, or you want to start, and notice inner resistance, in the form of the thought: "I can't, I don't want to, I don't know how to get this part right. . . . " That's your signal to . . .

TAKE A VACATION! Create a new condition in yourself, in your body. Get the juices flowing and find new energy for your writing.

Try any of these activities as an experiment, see if they help you start fresh.

1. Talk, talk, talk! about what you're doing. It gets you excited again, and emotion means more energy. Visit someone who encourages you, and talk about what you want to say. When ideas and phrases start coming, jot them down so you'll remember. Then, write nonstop.

2. If you jog, RUN. When you feel exhilarated, start typing what you want to say as fast as you can. Watch a page come pouring out.

3. Have someone massage your neck and shoulders (especially if you've been typing for hours) and close your eyes, trying to sense the contact of hand on skin, heat, blood flow. Look at the last page you wrote, and continue writing.

4. Shower or sauna especially trying to be aware of the surface of your skin. Whenever a discouraging thought occurs to you about what you're writing, simply sense the skin you're in: water on it, air on it, face, behind the knees. Later, try Experiment 1.

5. Dance up a sweat to your favorite music, whatever gets your body moving. Right away, ask yourself a question on paper, and answer it, writing quickly. Start anew with any sentence.

126

6. Charged up by good news? Now's the time to sit at the typewriter and do that part of your writing you've been putting off. All that energy will get you going strong.

7. Write your subject across the top of the page. Below it, write: "What's the story?" Put aside pad and pen, or move your chair away from the typewriter. Say: "Now I'm taking some time just for me." DO THE RELAXING EXERCISE (p. 16) for five minutes. Then write nonstop to the bottom of the page.

8. Lie down, your back and the soles of your feet flat on the floor, knees up, head raised just a few inches on a pillow or book. In this resting position, sense the whole length of your spine along the floor, and let your whole back relax there, supported by the floor. IMAGINE you're breathing in through different parts of your body, as if air could come in through your abdomen . . . thighs . . . scalp. . . . When you feel refreshed, try Experiment 28.

9. Take a walk. Let thoughts about writing remind you simply to become aware of each foot contacting the ground. SIT down with pad, and make a list of the points you want to cover in the piece you're writing.

10. Do any favorite activity that invigorates, yoga, stretching exercises, or jogging. Return again and again to the sensation of muscle stretching, and the shape your body takes. Later, write a question you want to answer and "talk" out on paper what you have to say.

11. Remind yourself you can write, then look at the sign or note you wrote after a flurry of satisfying activity. Close your eyes, and PICTURE how you were when you wrote that. Let a smile of confidence come up from inside. Smiling, open your eyes, and pick up your favorite pen (the one that has a nice "feel" as the ink flows onto the page): handwrite line after line.

12. Paint, pot, weave, sew, knit; repair or clean up something, trying to be aware, moment to moment, of the contact of hand and object. When you return to your

typewriter, start writing as if the whole story is there already, waiting to come out.

IF YOU'RE STUCK AT A PARTICULAR PLACE, sometimes you can ask yourself: What bothers me about this part? What does this piece need now?

Chuck M. has to present a writing sample to his prospective employer and wants to use an outline he wrote last year proposing a new program. He's uneasy about it "because it doesn't show my creativity or writing style." What can be added so it does? "A one-page description of how the program will benefit people." He writes at the top of a sheet: WHAT'S THIS PROGRAM ABOUT? HOW WILL IT BENEFIT PEOPLE? Writing nonstop to get going, he underlines highlights, and arranges them into a high-powered paragraph. Now he feels his writing sample shows off his organizational *and* creative abilities.

It helps *not* to think about writing as an ordeal. Trust that, with practice, you'll be clever and patient enough to get by any block. Make a pact with yourself that you'll never "force things" but instead will:

1. Recognize when you need a break and fresh energy.
2. Practice creating a new condition in yourself.
3. Try an experiment: write any first sentence or question just to get going.

The more you see how you can overcome being stuck, the more confident you become that you can write anything you want. You've done it once, and you'll do it again!

PART 4

TOWARD BECOMING
YOUR OWN BEST EDITOR

By now writing is coming easier to you, and it can be the same with revising.

It's not textbook English you're after. Talking in paragraphs brought out your unmistakable voice: the writing has drive and strength that comes from your natural way of expressing things. Your writing lives! and you're not about to formalize it to death.

You want only to tighten and sharpen what you have.

But how? If you're feeling it's going to be a chore, this is *not* the moment to begin, right? Set aside the work for a while. Come back when you're so curious you just have to take a look at all those pages you wrote.

And as you do, is there something you'd like to cross out? After hours of restraint, you may be eager to play editor. You see that this part sags, that you use a word too much, that another part sounds too. . . .

Editing can be such a relief! Now's your chance to unburden every sentence. Cross out without regret. The ultimate satisfaction comes when you type the final draft and feel you've got the exact words you want in the best order.

So, what stays and what goes?

"But everything looks good."

Here's one writer's description of what she thinks about while revising a page:

I look at the first sentence—does it interest me, move easily into the next? I see if there are any words that aren't pulling their weight, and cross them out. Perhaps I'll move around a word or two, put subject and verb closer together, put related words (modifiers and what they modify) next to each other. Is it clearer? I check to see if subject, verb, pronoun agree (all singular, or did I make my usual mistake of writing, "Everyone revises their own way" instead of "her own way?").

131

Move on to the next sentence. Does it follow? Is it an intensification of what just came? On the same subject, but giving more focus? I cross out every word I can, just to see if it moves better.

Perhaps a sentence is not quite right, but I'm not sure how to fix it. I write TK ("to come") in the margin. I'll go back to that later.

New paragraph. Do all the sentences in it relate to the same idea? Bracket the one that doesn't; find where to move it later; or omit. Do I end the paragraph with something that leads into the next? Do I need a word or phrase to begin this one that ties in with what just came?

One paragraph, one aspect? Extra words or sentences to cross out? Too many *it is* or *there is*: sounds dull? What voice is coming through? Put in a caret and insert a few words to make that point clearer. I write in an example.

New paragraph. Tied in to the last one? Something building? More specifics? Again, cut out anything that slows it down. Too flowery? What's the point here? Follow from the last paragraph? All sentences have to do with this same idea?

Here are a few things to help you become your own best editor.

While you're learning what to look for, rather than trying to do everything at once, you can read over your piece three times in this way:

1st reading: Listen for tone, locate rough spots.

2nd reading: Notice how you get from here to there.

3rd reading: Tighten and sharpen.

And when you've got a sentence that's convoluted and confusing, try Experiment 30 ("Say it over coffee").

FIRST: LISTEN FOR TONE, LOCATE ROUGH SPOTS

IMAGINE YOU'RE AN EDITOR, not the writer of this piece, and you're seeing it for the first time. It's your job to carve out the best of what's here.

Read out loud	**READ PAGE ONE OUT LOUD** to someone because you'll hear more. Ask your listener to answer these three questions (you may be able to answer them yourself):
	—What part do you remember? (Good!)
What stands out?	—What part do you need to hear again (didn't quite catch)? (Revise?)
What tone?	—In a few words, how does the voice coming through sound? (Sincere, informed? hedging? confused? boring? argumentative?)
What Purpose?	Decide on the purpose of this piece so you can check for appropriate tone of voice. Does the writing entertain or inform you? Try to get someone to do something? And if you're that someone, ideally what tone of voice would reach *you*?
	TRY TO IDENTIFY WHICH WORDS defeat that purpose: what group of words nags at you a little as you read? Usually you can hear rough spots the moment you say them aloud to someone.
Cross out or Bracket [ ] What Bothers You	Don't labor over these places now, unless you see right away what to omit or change. Just cross out in pencil, or bracket, what bothers you. Write TK (To Come) in the margin, and go on.
Who's Your Audience?	While reading for tone of voice and rough spots, you can also keep in mind who the piece is written for. A group of businessmen? An English teacher? Does it sound casual or formal? **WHAT PRONOUN** suits this piece?

For example, the reader of a formal report might respond better to a less "personal" tone. Go through and strike out all instances of "I'm writing this to," "I think,"

133

"You can see." Instead of *I* and *you*, use *one* and (the "editorial") *we*:

One finds striking examples of. . . .

We read that computers are. . . .

In this way, turn casual remarks into strong declarative sentences which make your opinion sound as if it's the reasonable point of view.

WHAT PRONOUN WORKS BEST?

If you're writing:	Try:	Example:
a "How to" article	you	First, you want to see . . .
an after-dinner speech	I, we	I saw we needed to try . . .
a paper for school	one	One finds in Emerson's . . .
a technical report	one	One accounts for such . . .
a story	I, he, she	I waited, but she never . . .

Stick with whatever pronoun works best and check to be sure you don't switch (from "I saw" to "You could see") halfway through the paragraph (see p. 11).

Did you notice any vague places, or clichés? For instance, you're talking about some historical event and write "and they got mad and did something about it." Isn't it vague? Who did what, specifically?

	You can write TK in the margin, and sharpen these places later. If you want to improve them now, supply specifics.
Vague?	Turn pronouns into nouns (names of persons, places, or things).
	Check facts, dates, spellings of proper nouns.
Clichés?	About clichés: in your haste it was easy to write "too funny for words." How funny? Look up *funny* in a thesaurus. Or show how people reacted.

134

Or you wrote: "We took everything but the kitchen sink." What's everything? "We took sleeping bags, rafts, insect repellent, charcoal briquets, and a baseball bat."

Supply
Specifics

Unless you're deliberately using clichés and vague phrases (to characterize a particular person who's speaking), give specifics.

SECOND: CHECK OUT YOUR BEGINNING, MIDDLE, END, AND LINKS BETWEEN PARTS

Beginning
—First sentence: ho-hum or tell-me-more?
—Start further along (where it heats up)?
—Does the reader know soon enough what it's about?
    Too soon? (Spoils the suspense)
    Too late? (Not sure, can't be bothered)

Middle
—Moving forward briskly? Going somewhere?
—Easy to follow? One paragraph, one aspect?
—Where does it sag, slow down, or stop?
    What if you cross out that whole part?
    Clearer?

CHECK YOUR ORDER OF PRESENTATION

1. *In pencil in the margin next to each paragraph JOT DOWN A FEW KEY WORDS that tell the main point*

2. *Does any sentence in that paragraph not apply? Omit, or move it?*

   To move a sentence, circle and mark it with a letter ("A"). Then write "INSERT A" where that sentence fits better.

3. *On a separate page, list your margin jottings. Does each point lead to the next?*

To move a paragraph, circle and mark it with a letter ("X"). Then write "INSERT X" where that paragraph belongs.

End
—Satisfying? Worth the time it takes?
—Is it clear why the piece is written?
—Does it leave you with a strong impression? What's that?
—Is this the place to stop? Gone on too long? Anti-climactic?
—Does the ending relate to the beginning?

You've looked at the beginning, middle, and end of your piece, and you have a phrase in pencil next to each paragraph giving its main point. Now look carefully at how you connect one paragraph to the next. Do you help your reader get from here to there?

Here are some ways to link paragraphs, so your piece holds together and moves well:

1. REPEAT A KEY WORD you used in Paragraph A when you write the opener for Paragraph B.

2. OPEN a paragraph with the next question in your reader's mind.
   (For example, you've told the reader that sour-dough bread is nutritious. In your next paragraph, you talk about a starter. Your lead-in might be, "How can you begin to make this wonderful food?")

3. USE A TRANSITIONAL word or phrase *unless the reader can follow* perfectly well without it. PRE-PARE your reader for what's coming:

an example:	For instance,
	For example,
a shift:	However,
	But
	Nevertheless,
	Or
	Up to this point

a reason:	Because, Therefore, In order to
another reason:	In addition, Also, Moreover,
a comparison:	Similarly, In the same way, In the same vein,
a contrast:	In contrast, Contrary to However, Unlike
another time:	Before Afterward, Then
a sequence:	First, Second, Third, Next,
a conclusion:	Thus, Therefore, To sum up,

4. LET the order within the PARAGRAPH keep the movement going in one direction.

(It's clear you're proceeding from left to right, from most obvious reason to least, from outside to inside.

5. LET THE WHITE ("BREATHING") SPACE between paragraphs show you're moving on to something else. New paragraph, new idea.

(Unless you're trying for a special effect, be sure to leave adequate white space on the page. It's difficult to read a long unbroken block of type.)

Ideally, transitions don't stand out but help parts of your piece stick together. Relationships between sentences and between paragraphs become clear.

NOTICE HOW YOU GET FROM HERE TO THERE

COHERENCE: Does one sentence lead naturally into the next? Can you easily follow from one paragraph to the next? Enough tie-ins and transitions? Something developing or building?

EMPHASIS: Are you rambling on, or do you show the relative importance of ideas? Is your main point clear? Does it stand out?

UNITY: Are you on a straight line from the beginning, through the middle, to the end? Do you keep to one purpose? Are you still writing in your natural voice?

THIRD: TIGHTEN AND SHARPEN

Tightening and sharpening,[1] taking out some words and substituting others: this is your final task. You've located rough spots, places that just don't sit well with you, sentences you want to improve with one aim in mind: to make your meaning clear.

Does each word pull its weight? What effect are you trying for? What may seem like flowery language may suit a parody. The fewest words, in plain English, may make a stronger letter. Every sentence, every word, should strengthen what you're saying.

So look for words, phrases, and sentences you can do without. When in doubt, cross it out, or at least experiment, listening to that section without those words. Do you like it better? Does it move well?

---

[1] Ken Macrorie uses these words to describe revising in his composition text *Telling Writing* (Hayden Book Co., 1970).

WHAT NEEDS TIGHTENING?

- Do I need these words?   • Is my writing better without them?

To practice becoming your own best editor, LOOK for the following places in your writing, and ⟨CIRCLE⟩. Suggestions for revising are in parentheses after each example.

—repeated words, phrases, ideas:

"he has never succeeded and always fails"	(say it once)
"let's *cooperate together* on this"	("let's cooperate")
"we *first began* the project"	("we began")
"⟨generate⟩ ideas and ⟨generate⟩ enthusiasm"	(word repeated)

—that, which, who:

"in spite of the fact that she is a woman who"	("although she")

—extra, little words (can you use two words instead of six?):

"meets with our approval"	("we approve")
"we are writing to ask that you send"	("please send")
"due to the fact that"	("because")

—jargon (phrases you wouldn't say over coffee; try plain English):

"enclosed herewith please find"	("Enclosed is"; "Here's")
"in the event that"	("if")
"effectuate the implementation of"	("implement" or "act on")

—jumbles of words which make you say "what?":

"Probably we should reconsider the assignment of control responsibilities as the proper development of guidelines for controls must reside with the most closely associated professional representative of the specific discipline or disciplinary area concerned with delivery" (Try Exp. 30!)

—dull verbs, one after another (is it monotonous?):
"There is no doubt that it is time for it to become a
reality" (Omit this whole phrase? Or cut out the
lead-in?) ("It's time")

—energetic verbs, one after another (is it too much?):
"Come here," he bellowed, and then chortled, "you
cutie." She wheezed, "I can't," then admonished,
"Don't come closer." (Use these verbs sparingly unless trying for a comic effect)

—adjectives and adverbs, too abundant (is it too flowery?):
"Immaculately white sailboats glided smoothly and
gracefully in stately majestic procession" (what
words can you cut?)

Now that you've noticed some rough spots, cut out every
word you don't need: is the sentence more brisk? stronger?
clearer?

If you're concerned about wordiness, here are some
examples of extra words you can cut from your writing.
In each instance, which word is unnecessary?

actual truth	necessary requirement
honest truth	first started
true facts	first began
deeds and actions	first and foremost
color green	postpone until later
right and proper	hour of noon
rules and regulations	patently obvious
small in size	pair of twins
assemble together	fall down
cooperate together	rise up
gather together	refer back
scrutinize carefully	city of Hartford
enclosed you will find	advance planning
narrow in width	consistent habit
	from a northeast direction

Tightening your writing means cutting out words you
don't need. Look over each sentence as if you want to

put it in the fewest words. Don't be attached to any word or phrase if you have an inkling you'd be better off if you cut it.

These are not rules to follow arbitrarily, just places to look when you want to revise. Remember you're still experimenting: do you like your tightened version better? Does it ring true to your experience or idea?

You notice the meaning may change when you rearrange. Perhaps your original sentence, with all those words, has a rhythm that expresses perfectly what you mean. Leave it. Context is crucial: when what's on the page suits your meaning, you already may have "the best words in the best order." For instance, you use "it is" a lot because you want to emphasize the word coming next. Or you string together five adjectives—and the sentence works wonderfully! Or you repeat a phrase, but each time change it slightly. "Repeat-and-vary" can be powerful, as in these final lines from Walt Whitman's "Song of the Open Road":

Allons! the road is before us!
It is safe—I have tried it—my own feet have
    tried it well—be not detain'd!

Let the paper remain on the desk unwritten, and
    the book on the shelf unopen'd!
Let the tools remain in the workshop! let the
    money remain unearn'd!
Let the school stand! mind not the cry of the teacher!
Let the preacher preach in his pulpit! let the lawyer
    plead in the court, and the judge expound the law.

Camerado, I give you my hand!
I give you my love more precious than money,
I give you myself before preaching or law;
Will you give me yourself? will you come travel with me?
Shall we stick by each other as long as we live?

WHAT NEEDS SHARPENING?

Circle the following words in your writing and see if revising helps.

—*is, was, were* (forms of the verb "to be" used too often)

Here's how to switch to the "active" voice:

	"Active" verbs
sounds could (be) heard →	we *heard* sounds
it (is) important to study	one *should study*
there (is) no problem	no problem *exists*

Write a story like this: ("Once Upon a Was")

"Once there (was) a man who (was) rich. He (was) six feet tall. He (was) fond of eating berries...."

Then rearrange sentences, and use "active" verbs. "Once I *knew* a rich man. He *stood* six feet tall. He *liked* to eat berries...."

Note: You need not omit every instance of "it is" or "there is." In a scientific report, you may prefer to use them to avoid "I" (see p. 98).

—dull verbs, such as *go, move, have, make*

If you're writing a story especially, look up your "dull" verb in a thesaurus. *Go* might yield *shuffle, limp, saunter, strut.* Does one of these suit the passage?

Instead of: This room (has) the look of a deserted barn.

Write: This room *looks* like....

Instead of: He (moved) with difficulty into the room.

Write: He *hobbled* into the room.

Note: Don't overdo (see p. 140 about too many "energetic" verbs).

—colorless phrases which explain rather than show

> Instead of: He (was) feeling rather bad.
> Show it: He slumped in his chair.
>
> Show by means of posture, movement, gesture.

—"hedge" words: sort of, kind of, possibly, somewhat, relatively

> Instead of: Terry (was) (sort of) a saint to me, and (somewhat) of an influence on me in a (relatively) short time.
> Write: I idolized Terry; in a short time, she changed my life.
>
> Take the risk of sounding sure. Is it stronger?

—negative phrases ("did not") when you could find a stronger positive phrasing

> Instead of: He (did not) have much confidence in books on writing, and (did not) think them very useful.
> Try this: He *distrusted* books on writing, and thought them *useless*.

NOTE: These are not rules, but ways to experiment until you find just the phrasing you want to suit your tone and meaning.

Experiment 30
Sounds confusing? Say it over coffee

When you're not sure how to revise a confusing or wordy sentence, try this with someone:

1. READ ALOUD the sentence you want to make clear. LOOK UP.

2. Your friend asks, "What do you mean?"

3. SAY "I MEAN . . . " and say what you mean straight out. (*Don't* look down at the page.)

4. WRITE down what you just said—that's it! Try it (or something like it) in the passage.

Did you notice
  —that looking at the page, and moving words around, sometimes doesn't help you make the passage clearer?
  —how useful it is simply to lift your head, and "talk out" just what you mean?
  —that when you tell someone what you mean, you say it simply and clearly?

A QUICK CHECK LIST

Wordy	*Cut out extra words?*
or	*Say it just once?*
Concise?	*Brisk or rambling? Suits your meaning?*
Active	*Too many "it is" and "there is?"*
Verbs or	*"We heard them" (active) or "they could be*
Passive?	*heard" (passive)—which works best?*
Jargon or	*Say it in two words instead of eight?*
Plain	*Sounds pompous, or honest?*
English?	*Would you "say it over coffee?"*
Show	*Vivid sensory details?*
or	*Concrete specifics and telling examples?*
Explain?	*Energetic verbs?*
Flows	*Logical progression from here to there?*
or	*Clear transitions so you can follow easily?*
Falters?	*Any leaps or gaps?*

WHEN TO PROOFREAD, AND WHY IT PAYS

You've been working for hours and have read each page so many times you don't notice typos or spelling mistakes. LET IT REST for a while! You need to come to it with new eyes.

When you're ready to proofread, look at each sentence. There's no hurry. Remember you owe it to the quality of your work to catch those errors in spelling, typing, punctuation, and grammar. Minor mistakes distract your reader, make her lose faith in you as someone worth reading. Even a pencilled-in correction is better than an error.

How does the page look? Adequate margins? Not crammed, but easy to read?

Look at each sentence for spelling, typos, and punctuation.

—CHECK A DICTIONARY to spell any word you're not sure of.
—CHECK A GRAMMAR HANDBOOK to find out what's correct.

Such as: the spelling of words you wonder about. *Separate* or *seperate*? *Guarantee* or *guarentee*? Which spelling of a sound-alike, *principle* or *principal*? *Affect* or *effect*? What is the past tense of *lie*? *Lay, laid* or *lain*? Where does the apostrophe go in "Jones's house?"

When you come to the end of a line, how do you divide a word correctly? Break it where? See a dictionary.

WHAT ABOUT SPELLING, PUNCTUATION, AND GRAMMAR?

Some Common Mistakes to Watch for:

Spelling
IT'S or ITS? → *IT'S* always means *IT IS*
(Memorize: It's time for its bath)

YOU'RE or → *YOU'RE* always means YOU ARE
YOUR?

THEY'RE,	→	*THEY'RE* always means THEY ARE
THEIR,	→	as in "their book" (whose?)
THERE?	→	as in "over there" (where?)
A LOT	→	is two words (look up *alot*: no such word)
ALL RIGHT	→	is two words.

Punctuation

If you're not sure when to use a comma or semi-colon, look in a handbook for the rule. Watch for these places:

1. Don't put a comma between subject and verb.

   WRONG: Another fantasy of mine, is to. . . .

→ RIGHT: Another fantasy of mine is to. . . .

2. Don't use only a comma when you need a stronger "stop" between two long complete sentences[1].

   WRONG: I was confident about meeting him, I'd heard he was sympathetic.

→ RIGHT: I was confident about meeting him. I'd heard he was sympathetic.

(or)

I was confident about meeting him; I'd heard. . . .

If you have a series of short, complete sentences, you can use commas, such as:

→ RIGHT: I paced, I wept, I moaned.

Here's a sentence to remember about the semi-colon.

→ RIGHT: The *semi-colon* **is** a useful mark of punc-

             s.   v.

             ↓

tuation; *it* **connects** two related complete

    s.   v.

sentences.

3. Don't run together two complete sentences when you need a "stop" between them. (Put in a period, semi-colon, or colon, *not* a comma.)

---

[1] A complete sentence has a *subject* (person, place, or thing) and a **verb** (shows action or state of being). The verb form "agrees" with the subject (that is, both singular or both plural).

The *book* **is** finished. *John* **ran** home. (*You*) **Watch** it!

  s. v.   s. v.   s.   v.

WRONG: Their plans were exciting/they looked forward to a month in Bhutan.

→ RIGHT: Their plans were exciting. They ...

(or)   exciting; they ...

(or)   exciting: they ...

Grammar and sentence structure

Check for these:

☐ "Danglers" (the phrase you open with is not close enough to the word it describes: confusion results)

WRONG: *Hiding his nuts* in the tree, *John* watched the squirrel. (who hid what?)

→ RIGHT: John watched the squirrel hiding his nuts in the tree.

WRONG: Swimming in the sea, the waves nearly drowned us. (were the waves swimming?)

→ RIGHT: *Swimming* in the sea, *we* nearly drowned in the waves.

Whenever you begin a sentence with an "—ing" phrase, be sure the word coming right after the comma is the person or thing that's hurrying, swimming, or hiding.

Watch for places where you need to PUT RELATED WORDS CLOSE TOGETHER, next to each other.

☐ "Modifiers" (adjectives and adverbs) not close enough to the word they modify or describe

WRONG: He only found two arrowheads.

→ RIGHT: He found *only two* arrowheads. (How many? Only two.)

☐ Subject so far from the verb it's confusing

UNCLEAR: The boys wanting to see a deer and hoping that if they walked very quietly would not scare away the animals put on their sneakers.

→ CLEAR: The boys put on their sneakers. They wanted. . . .

☐ Sentence fragments (You can use an incomplete sentence for effect. Otherwise, try to write complete sentences.)

INCOMPLETE: The wedding present *that got him present* started in pottery. (verb missing: what did the present *do?* what about it?)

→ COMPLETE: The wedding present got him started in pottery.

(or)

The wedding present that got him started in pottery *proved* to be the best gift he ever received.

☐ Lack of "agreement" among subject, verb, and possessive pronoun (all singular? all plural?)

WRONG: Everyone has their way of working.
  (*Everyone* is singular, but *their* is plural)

→ RIGHT: Everyone has *her* way of working. (or)
  Everyone has *his* way of working.

Writing quickly, we make this mistake a lot, especially with the words: *everybody, anybody, no one, nobody.* Usually, all take a singular verb (has, goes, is) and a singular possessive pronoun (his, her).

There are exceptions. When the word referred to is plural in *meaning* (although singular in form), it can take a plural pronoun:

→ RIGHT: Everybody was at the party, and *they* all stayed late to sing *their* songs.
  They show that many were involved.

Do you need to locate the subject, verb, and pronoun? Try this:

Cross out phrases beginning "*to* the ___, *in* the ___,"
^{preposition} ^{prep.}

"of . . . " (prepositional phrases never contain the subject).

Find the verb. If the subject is singular, is the verb?

Memorize: *Each* ~~of the girls~~ has (her) own room.
^{s.} ^{prep. phrase}

("each, has, her": all singular)

☐ Lack of parallelism when using combinations such as "either . . . or . . . ," "both . . . and . . . ," "not only . . . but also"[1]

WRONG: Either you find an example or weaken your case.

→ RIGHT: You either find an example or weaken your case.

Check what part of speech (verb, noun, pronoun?) comes directly after *either* and after *or*. Try for the same part of speech:

either *verb*   Either *find* . . .
                                            ^{v.}
or   *verb*   or *weaken* . . .
                                            ^{v.}

WRONG: You not only should check punctuation but also grammar.

→ RIGHT: You should check not only punctuation, but also grammar.

not only *noun*   . . . not only *punctuation*
                                                      ^{n.}
but also *noun*   but also *grammar.*
                                                      ^{n.}

Here's one more example of KEEPING THINGS PARALLEL.

WRONG: I can show you how *to get* going, how *to carry* on, how *to revise,* and *punctuation.* (3 verbs and a noun)

----

[1] coordinating conjunctions

149

→ RIGHT: I can show you how *to get* going, how *to carry* on, how *to revise*, and how *to punctuate*.

→ EVEN BETTER (TIGHTENED): I can show you how to get going, carry on, revise, and punctuate. (4 verbs in parallel form)

If these common mistakes and ways to correct them are totally unfamiliar, you may need to improve your writing skills. Find a composition handbook that seems clear and easy to follow: study what you need to know. Some have "diagnostic tests" to pinpoint difficulties. Or ask for a programmed book that helps you teach yourself the fundamentals one small step at a time.

WRITING SAMPLES REVISED

Or should this section be entitled, "Revised Writing Samples?"

Recommending a change of words is suggesting a change of meaning, however slight. Ask yourself: does the new version better suit your tone and meaning? Does it place the emphasis where you want it? Does the piece move better?

Revising is experimenting: finding just the right words and putting them just the right way, with nothing extra or incorrect.

The writing samples below reflect this writer's particular way of revising. Common grammatical errors are included, and corrected. Words are bracketed which could be left out so the piece "moves well." Where appropriate, the reasoning behind the revisions is included.

Sample A: From a report or article introducing a newly patented process:

[OMIT UNNECESSARY WORDS]

don't repeat *every*

run together sentences (comma not strong enough: need a period.)

better (and fewer) words

dangler: did the process recognize this or did the corporation?

don't repeat *handle;* be more specific

waste, the subject, agrees with *is,* the verb

products needs *are*

better word

putting a colon to introduce the list

[It is estimated that] every (E.)

[single] person in the U.S. [today]

makes from three to ten pounds of

garbage [every day] *daily* (M) municipalities

[and towns have found themselves]

paying over 3.2 billion dollars

annually [in order to rid themselves] *to dispose*

of 3.6 billion dollars' worth of

paper alone. Recognizing the need

for a better way to handle garbage, *Biocel Corporation developed*

a newly patented non-polluting

process for [handling garbage has] *recovering every bit*

of material we now dis-

card. been developed by Biocel Corpora-

tion. [Pound for pound, [each part of *all*

the incoming waste [streams] *is* are

turned into products which

are

is in great demand in today's

marketplaces

[business world.] Biocel's products

are the basic raw materials of

modern industry: [such as] ferrous

and non-ferrous metals, aluminum,

glass, high-nutrient fertilizer,

and high-quality long-fiber paper

pulp.

COMMENT: "Extra" words have been bracketed (to be omitted): does the paragraph move briskly when revised this way?

Sample B: A student's essay

Try rewriting the short essay below. It's great practice for learning how to become your own best editor. Could you have found the mistakes? Even if the piece were grammatically correct, what's needed here?

ABOUT REVISING SOMEONE ELSE'S WRITING: Two much red penciling can be demoralizing. Avoid handing the writer a page like the one below covered with notations of what's wrong, with not a word about what's good in the piece. Point out what's appealing: vivid details, potential for expansion and development. How can the writer tap her own experience and present it in a lively way? Also useful is a person-to-person talk for a few minutes to encourage the writer even as you help her find and correct mistakes. Once you point out a weak place, she may know already what's wrong and even how to make it right. It's useful for you to be clear about the following:

(1) what stage is the paper at? (rough, first, final draft? ideas gelled yet?)
(2) what one thing does this writer do well? (tell her!)
(3) what one thing is needed most now? (what would move the piece along to the next stage?).

Stressing poor mechanics or organization at a stage in the writing when what's lacking is sufficient material might discourage the writer. Save those comments for a later conference when the piece is further along. Help the writer become sensitive to what's needed at every stage: generate more ideas? notice beginning, middle, and end, order of presentation? check each sentence for grammar and punctuation? tighten and sharpen? proofread carefully?

OWNING A CAR

From my experience in owning a
car, (it) has many advantages.
[Therefore, I would <u>associate a car</u>
<u>as being a positive factor</u>.]

Having a car, gives (you) a sense
of freedom and power. Freedom of
doing things on (your) own, without
any <u>opposing factors</u> from others.
Going places in (your) own car
without any <u>questions</u> [to your
whereabouts.]

The effect of power, that
lingers when owning a car of your
own symbolizes the authoritative
factor that most teenagers crave.

In experiencing this effect of
power, (it) can also <u>create</u> much
de'struction.
Destruction in a^(the) sense of harming
oneself, as well as others.

Handwritten margin notes (left):

"it" refers to what?
The opening phrase
needs to modify
"I" not "it". Re-write
with "I" as the
subject of the sentence:
"I find...."

No comma between
subject and verb

Shift in person from
"I" to "you". Stick with
"I", "my", "me" (first
person).

my own

Why a new paragraph?
no comma

This sentence
doesn't make sense
Stilted language. How
would you say what
you mean (out loud)?
Try that.

Create... destruction?
These are opposites

Don't repeat
destruction

Like what exactly?
What's destructive
about driving cars?
What can cars mean to people?
How do people use them? Give examples which are vivid.

Handwritten margin notes (right):

What about "it"?
Find a more
specific title.

OMIT. Awkwardly
phrased. Adds
nothing. Mis-using
the word associate.
Positive factor
in what?

← Incomplete
sentences

Like what
exactly?

[Omit extra Words]
Avoid awkward
combination of words

Expand. Can you
give an example?

"It" refers to what?
Who experiences?
You need "I" as
the subject of
the sentence.

Combine as one
sentence
Sentence fragment
as is

cause?

153

Along with the many advantages
and disadvantages [spoken about],

(their) are many more disadvantages
[that I would like to focus on].

In general, the price of cars,
the price of gas and just the basic

conditions which one has to endure
when owning a car.∧

Pollution is a great disadvan-
tage [when owning a car]. But this
society is so automobile oriented

(its) really impossible to cut back
on pollution.

Although, if (their) is cooperation, (their) may be one alternative⊙

car pool(ings).

↙ Car pooling F[from my own ex-
does
perience (dose) lower the percentage

and
of air pollution [as well as] helps

save on the price of gas.

[Through the previous analysis⊙
on automobiles⊙] I can now conclude

that] with the proper understanding

[of automobiles] and the basic steps
to handle them. There should be no
problem with owning one.

COMMENT: It's hard to believe that this writer expresses herself coherently and pointedly when she speaks out loud. Something drastic happens when it comes time to put ideas into words on paper. In place of the easy flow of speech with its vivid personal details, there are confusing stilted lines like "the effect of power . . . symbolizes the authoritative factor that most teenagers crave" which doesn't make sense. Sentences are incomplete (often lacking a verb). Paragraphs are incomplete (and all the same length, short, choppy), lacking a main point followed by supporting details (statistics, examples, incidents, anecdotes). Yet surely the writer could tell out loud what she's read or what happened to her that led to these statements. She needs more material and a more orderly presentation, a sense of something building, from opening question to concluding statement. What would be a logical arrangement of materials here?

THE QUESTION
DISADVANTAGES
ADVANTAGES
(or vice versa, depending on
which she were stressing)
THE ANSWER

She should keep in mind "ONE ASPECT, ONE PARAGRAPH," and be able to say in a phrase the MAIN POINT of each paragraph.

"Talking" nonstop on paper would help her generate an easier flow of words and an abundance of supporting detail.

HOW WOULD YOU BEGIN TO REWRITE THIS PIECE?

Try this:

1. Take three sheets of paper and write a question across the top of each.
    What are the advantages of owning a car?
    What are the disadvantages?
    What's been my experience with cars?

2. Write (nonstop) cach page.
3. Underline highlights.
4. Jot down briefly how the essay will develop, like this:
   1st paragraph: Ask the question your essay will answer, such as

   _____ ?

   2nd: Main point is _____
        (such as, first disadvantage?)
        Supporting details _____
        (an incident, statistic, personal experience)
   3rd: Main point _____
        (second disadvantage?)
        Supporting details _____
   4th: Main point _____
        ("In contrast," then give first advantage?)
        Support _____
   5th: Main point _____
        ("Finally," then give second advantage?)
        Support _____
   6th: ("Thus") Tie in with opening question. Sum up, conclude.

Here's how a revised version might begin, drawing on specific details from the writer's experience.

A CAR OF MY OWN: IS IT WORTH IT?

When my Dad handed me the keys to my very own Chevy, I lit up. What did it mean to me? Freedom! Coming and going as I pleased! Now, after two months of gas lines, repair bills, and five flat tires, I realize there are disadvantages as well.

It costs so much today to own a car. This summer, I couldn't believe it when the digits on the gas pump rolled past a dollar fifty a gallon. . . .

Sample C: A letter of complaint

Your address
Date

Mr. Restaurant Manager (by name)
Blook's Restaurant
Address

Dear

[Omit --
Extra words?]
Tone not right

How about opening
with something
more appealing
to the reader,
that'll still get
the job done?

[I am writing this letter to you
to complain] about what happened to
my husband and [I] when we were

to ... me

eating at your restaurant last
Saturday night. [You know,] your
place is our favorite place to eat,

← Open with
this

so we were quite distressed when we
had such an unpleasant experience.

Too much
colines
Condense

When we arrived, we were
seated between two tables of heavy
smokers. My eyes started to tear,
and when I asked one of the women
if she would please blow the smoke
in the other direction, she got
very angry. There didn't seem to
be any other tables available that
I could see, so we just gulped down
our food and left. Our evening out
was ruined.

Ask as a
direct question
about doing
this?
Sentence runs
on too long.

I think you run the risk of
losing a lot of business unless you
consider setting aside a non-
smokers section in your restaurant
because I know I am reluctant to go
back unless I can be assured of
having a leisurely enjoyable meal.

possessive:
smokers'
section

Sincerely yours,

157

Here's a possible rewrite which might be more effective in tone:

Dear   ,

Block's is our favorite restaurant, and I've got a suggestion for you that should improve business. Have you considered setting up a nonsmokers' section?

I ask because last Saturday night we were seated between two tables of heavy smokers. There was nowhere to move, so we had to put up with the smoke, rush through dinner, and leave.

I'm sure a nonsmokers' section would make your restaurant more pleasant: we want to be able to keep dining at Block's! Will you try it out?

Sincerely yours,

Sample D: From a story

Left margin notes (handwritten):

Condense so the emphasis stays on Sandra's striking entrance.

A colon might set off how she looked

Not every noun needs a modifier

Too flowery?

A bit too much? Take out some of the description.

"Flows better with revised word order.

No need to say both "make-up"

Better words? Closer to your meaning?

Who's speaking? Put in a sentence to begin the paragraph, such as, SANDRA WALKED OVER TO THE TABLE. "Warren..."

Main text (typewritten, with handwritten edits):

When Sandra walked into the dining room of the restaurant, [her *Price in tow?* handsome husband Price was trailing behind her.] All heads turned: to look at her. She was striking in her red suit [*chic* chicly out, and] slit up the front to show the inside of her [~~her~~ dark-stockinged] thigh. A [*small* ~~tiny~~] red cocktail hat, [perched jauntily and] tilted slightly over her forehead, *brought out* ~~showed off~~ the red in [*flowing auburn*] her [~~brown~~] shoulder-length hair. She [*wore a lot* had on a great deal of] make-up, rouge, ~~and~~ eye shadow and mascara, but no one [*could fault her* would question it:] surely this svelte woman was a model.

     "Warren, Grace. How are you this evening? Been waiting long?

Right margin notes (handwritten):

[OMIT extra words]

Don't repeat show. Check a thesaurus for another verb? Look up red and brown also; maybe there's a better word.

159

Where was the chair? Try to keep related words close to each other:

Use contractions to sound more like real talking:

Too strenuous? "purred," then "oozed". Omit.

"question in her face"? on her face?

Not necessary so omit

Would he say "My..."?

Not necessary so omit (rather than overdo)

No need to write "he answered". We know Warren is talking.

Punctuation goes inside quotation marks.

Add this to make it clearer.

Grace's questioning

its = it is

you're = you are

stood up, and
Warren pulled out the chair for Sandra next to him. [He answered,] ''Our train was on time, so we were early. We've [We have] ordered cocktails already.''

''You look lovely tonight, Grace,'' Grace'', Sandra purred. She didn't mean a word of it. ''You two make such an attractive couple,'' she oozed.

Grace smiled. She was surprised when Price sat down next rather than Sandra to her. He noticed [the question in look her face], and muttered, ''Jeni will be joining us if she can make it. We'll [We will] leave a place for her next to her mother.''

Warren had no sooner sat down again, then Sandra's hand was [he felt] on his thigh.

Price didn't waste any time either. [He offered,] ''Grace, dear. its so good to see you. My, how you've bloomed these past months.''

[She retorted,] ''Your looking well also, Price.''

160

Here's Sample D, with extra words removed:

When Sandra walked into the dining room of the restaurant, Price in tow, all heads turned: she was striking in her chic red suit slit up the front to show the inside of her thigh. A small red cocktail hat, tilted slightly over her forehead, brought out the red in her flowing auburn hair. She wore a lot of rouge, eye shadow and mascara, but no one could fault her: surely this svelte woman was a model.

Sandra walked over to the table. "Warren, Grace. How are you this evening? Been waiting long?"

Warren stood up, and pulled out the chair next to him for her. "Our train was on time, so we were early. We've ordered cocktails already."

"You look lovely tonight, Grace," Sandra purred. She didn't mean a word of it. "You two make such an attractive couple."

Grace smiled. She was surprised when Price sat down next to her rather than Sandra. He noticed Grace's questioning look, and muttered, "Jeni will be joining us if she can make it. We'll leave a place for her next to her mother."

Warren had no sooner sat down again when he felt Sandra's hand on his thigh.

Price didn't waste any time either. "Grace dear, it's so good to see you. How you've bloomed these past months."

"You're looking well also, Price."

APPRECIATE YOUR FINAL DRAFT

You did it! And you can do it again.

What a wealth of material you've put together. Your persistence paid off. Doesn't it feel good to finish something?

Congratulations. Now, treat yourself: CELEBRATE!

Glossary

ABSTRACT. (1) n. A summary giving the main points. (2) adj. Theoretical, general, indefinite (rather than concrete and specific), such as a concept, or a quality apart from a particular object (e.g. blackness, freedom, honesty).

ARGUMENT. A reason offered for or against something. A proof designed to persuade.

BIBLIOGRAPHY. An alphabetical list of all books and articles read or consulted, including but not limited to those appearing in footnotes. A *bibliography* always goes at the end of a paper.

The correct form for a book is:

> Shaw, Fran. *30 Ways to Help You Write*. New York: Bantam Books, 1980.

The correct form for an article is:

> Shaw, Fran. "Writing Free-flow to Build Momentum," *Writer's Newsletter*, X,2 (April, 1980), 11-14.

CAUSE AND EFFECT. *Cause* refers to the reason something happened. *Effect* refers to the result of what happened. For example:

His harsh words made her cry.
cause   effect

CHARACTER. A being, person, or individual in a story.

CHARACTERIZATION. The creation of an imaginary person or being. *Characterization* provides details of posture, gesture, speech, actions, thoughts, physical appearance, reactions, wishes and dreams.

CLIMAX. The turning point in a story, when something is resolved.

CONCRETE. adj. Tangible, specific, perceivable to the senses. *Concrete* details have to do with actual things or events. Some *concrete* details are: a dripping faucet, a red poinsettia, cinnamon toast, peacock feathers.

CONFLICT. The meeting of opposing forces or persons. *Conflict* involves a battle for mastery, a clash of personalities, interests, opinions, ideals or goals.

163

CONTEXT. Words, phrases, or sentences coming before and after a given passage. These words, phrases, or sentences throw light on the meaning of the passage.

CRISIS. A crucial or decisive moment in a struggle when things change for better or worse. A *crisis* leads to the climax.

DESCRIPTION. A *description* shows how something looks, sounds, smells, tastes, feels to the touch, and conveys a picture or impression through the use of sensory specifics; vivid pertinent details are selected and shaped for a certain effect.

DIALOGUE. A conversation; a spoken exchange of ideas, feelings, and information. *Dialogue* reveals characters, and advances the action of a story.

DISSERTATION. A formal essay or thesis treating a subject extensively.

DOCUMENTATION. Supporting material or evidence, cited in footnotes and listed in a bibliography, to back up statements.

EDITORIAL WE. The use of the pronoun *we* instead of *I* in reports, speeches, and letters (e.g. "We at Con Oil feel a responsibility to . . .").

EFFECTIVENESS. Getting the results you want, creating the desired impression. *Effectiveness* requires communicating in a clear way.

EMPHASIS. Stressing an idea or word to show its importance.

EMPHASIZING. Making something stand out.

EXPOSITION. Explaining something, defining or analyzing it, in an essay.

FICTION. An imagined or invented composition or story that never happened.

FLASHBACK. (1) n. A scene or incident that happened earlier. (2) vb. To *flashback* is to go from the present moment to a prior time.

FOOTNOTE. A listing of information about any document cited in your essay. Direct quotations, someone else's ideas, and passages from others' works must be footnoted when you cite them as examples and supporting material. *Footnotes* go at the bottom of the page on which the material is used, or as a list of "Notes" at the end of the paper.

[1] Fran Shaw, *30 Ways to Help You Write* (New York: Bantam Books, 1980), p. 125.

HAIKU. A Japanese poem of seventeen syllables. A *haiku* expresses a heightened moment of awareness.

HERO or **HEROINE.** Usually the main character in a story, possessing some special quality, strength, or ability.

IMAGE. A likeness of something or someone. An *image* vividly represents physical characteristics or a quality of life (e.g. a man might be described as "a great lumbering bear," a woman's eyes as "pools of light").

INDEX. An alphabetical list of topics discussed in a book. An *index* appears at the back of a book with page numbers showing where the topics appear.

JARGON. The vocabulary of a special group or profession. A special private language, not common speech. *Jargon* can also mean unintelligible language (gobbledygook, gibberish, "business-ese," "legal-ese"). The following phrase is an example of *jargon*: "endeavor to ascertain what was heretofore deemed unobtainable."

JOURNAL. A daily, personal record of what happened, what you read and thought or felt.

MOOD. The prevailing emotional state, atmosphere or tone in a piece of writing. *Mood* is conveyed through selected details of what a character sees or thinks or feels.

MOTIVATION. Why a character does what he does. *Motivations* are the causes, reasons, explanations supplied to show what drives a character.

NARRATION, NARRATIVE. An account of what happened.

NON-FICTION. Writing based on facts and reality. *Non-fiction* is not imagined or invented. Examples of non-fictional writing are autobiography, biography, science and history books.

OUTLINE. n. A plan or sketch of the main points of a piece of writing. In an *outline,* the main ideas are arranged in an organized sequence.

PLAIN ENGLISH. Spoken English. To use *plain English,* write as if you were talking, rather than writing. Plain English is the opposite of jargon and is never stilted, pompous, or flowery.

PLOT. A series of events and actions, causes and effects, arranged to advance a story.

POINT OF VIEW. The angle, such as a physical location in time and space, from which something is seen, or an attitude toward a subject. *Point of view* also refers to writing in the first person ("I"), second person ("you"), or third person ("he sat . . ."). "Third person omniscient point of view" refers to the all-knowing narrator, who can say what's in the minds of the characters (e.g. Grace sat on the beach, wondering if David would come).

RÉSUMÉ. A summary of your experience, education, qualities, and qualifications. When you apply for a job, you present your *résumé* to the prospective employer.

RISING ACTION. Events in a struggle leading to a crisis and to the climax or turning point of a story.

SATIRE. Humorous writing exposing human follies. *Satire* can ridicule gently or savagely.

SCENE. A single situation or dialogue in a piece of writing. The *scene* is also the place where something happens.

SETTING. The locale or time period in which something takes place.

SHORT STORY. A unified short narrative, usually under 10,000 words. A *short story* generally tries to create a single strong impression.

SKETCH. (1) v. To jot down details, main points. (2) n. A brief outline or short descriptive essay.

STORY. A narrative account of what happened, either true or fictitious.

STRUCTURE. How something is arranged or put together. The *structure* is the framework of a story, article, essay, or poem, with all the parts in a certain order.

STYLE. A way of using language which expresses the spirit and personality of the writer. *Style* is your unique way of putting thoughts and impressions into words. Your style might be "breezy" or "upbeat" or "spellbinding."

SUMMARY. A short, comprehensive statement of the main points.

SUSPENSE. Uncertainty and tension about "what happens next?"

SYMPATHY. Feelings of concern and compassion for a character.

TECHNIQUE. The method used to achieve a certain effect, the "how" of writing well. A writer's *techniques* might include varying the length of sentences and paragraphs, or using comparisons, or dialogue.

THEME. The main idea or message. A short essay is sometimes called a *theme*.

THESIS. A theory or proposition to be proven, involving research and documentation. A *thesis* is also a dissertation or long essay exploring a subject extensively.

TONE. (1) Modulation of the voice (e.g. a "demanding" tone of voice). (2) The manner of expression which reveals a writer's attitude toward her subject or reader. For example, a writer's tone might be sarcastic, or inspirational, or condescending.

TRANSITION. A way of getting from one point to another in what you're writing. A *transition* might be a word or passage connecting one part with the next.

UNITY. A totality of related parts held together by some organizing principle, method of presentation, or dominant impression. When your writing has *unity*, there is a sense of the parts fitting together to form a whole.

A Brief Selection of Books
for the Writer

Appelbaum, J. and Evans, N. *How to Get Happily Published*. New York: Harper & Row, 1978.

Two professional editors offer candid advice about selling your writing, also about self-publishing. Fine list of resources (books, organizations) to meet the writer's needs.

Elbow, Peter. *Writing Without Teachers*. New York: Oxford University Press, 1977.

How freewriting can help you "unblock" your writing; why it's useful to write first, edit later. How to set up a teacherless writing class.

Flesch, Rudolph. *On Business Communications*. New York: Barnes and Noble, 1974.

Writing concise letters and reports without jargon.

Glazier, T. F. *The Least You Should Know About English*. New York: Holt, Rinehart, and Winston, 1979.

One grammatical point at a time, with abundant exercises for practice, and answers at the back.

Hall, Donald. *Writing Well*. Boston: Little, Brown and Company, 1976.

How words (i.e. parts of speech) function. Common problems, and how to correct mistakes. For students in composition classes.

Hills, Rust. *Writing in General and the Short Story in Particular*. New York: Bantam Books, 1979.

Highly readable survey of techniques used in writing stories and novels.

Macrorie, Ken. *Telling Writing*. Rochelle Park, New Jersey: Hayden Book Co., 1970.

A new way to teach composition, using freewriting to generate material. Many suggestions for how to get going, and tighten and sharpen your writing. How to give useful feedback to another writer.

MLA Style Sheet. New York: Modern Language Association, 1970. *MLA Handbook*. New York: Modern Language Association, 1977.

Includes sample footnotes and bibliography.

Writers at Work: The Paris Review Interviews, ed. Malcolm Cowley (first, second, and third series), ed. George Plimpton (fourth series). New York: Viking Press.

How well-known writers approach writing. Includes sample pages from works in progress.

Index

ABOUT THE AUTHOR

DR. FRAN WEBER SHAW has been writing professionally since she was eight years old. While in high school, she was a regular columnist for a Hartford newspaper and received a number of awards for her writing. After graduating *magna cum laude* from Barnard College, she earned an M.A. in English literature from Stanford University and a Ph.D. from the Union Graduate School. A former Madison Avenue copywriter, Dr. Shaw's articles and poetry appear often in a variety of publications. She has taught creative writing and literature at several universities, and is presently Assistant Professor of English at the Stamford branch of the University of Connecticut where her duties include the coordination of the writing program. Dr. Fran Shaw is busy working on her first novel.

LEARNING TO WRITE AND ENJOYING IT

Books that can help you improve your ability to communicate. The interested beginning writer will find valuable direction and hints about how to write more efficiently and creatively.

Facts at Your Fingertips!

☐	34059	A SIGH OF RELIEF (A Large Format Book)	$12.95
☐	34057	THE COLLEGE SURVIVAL KIT (A Large Format Book)	$4.95
☐	23595	THE ART OF MIXING DRINKS	$3.50
☐	23061	EVERYTHING YOU ALWAYS WANTED TO KNOW ABOUT FIRE SAFETY	$2.95
☐	20832	THE PUBLICITY HANDBOOK	$3.50
☐	22573	THE BANTAM BOOK OF CORRECT LETTER WRITING	$3.50
☐	23909	THE COMMON SENSE BOOK OF KITTEN AND CAT CARE	$3.50
☐	23522	GETTING THINGS DONE	$3.50
☐	23474	AMY VANDERBILT'S EVERYDAY ETIQUETTE	$3.95
☐	14954	SOULE'S DICTIONARY OF ENGLISH SYNONYMS	$2.95
☐	20085	THE BANTAM NEW COLLEGE SPANISH & ENGLISH DICTIONARY	$2.75
☐	23111	THE GUINNESS BOOK OF WORLD RECORDS 21st ed.	$3.95
☐	20957	IT PAYS TO INCREASE YOUR WORD POWER	$2.95
☐	14890	THE BANTAM COLLEGE FRENCH & ENGLISH DICTIONARY	$2.75
☐	20298	THE FOOLPROOF GUIDE TO TAKING PICTURES	$3.50
☐	23393	SCRIBNER/BANTAM ENGLISH DICTIONARY	$2.95
☐	22975	WRITING AND RESEARCHING TERM PAPERS	$2.95

Prices and availability subject to change without notice.

Buy them at your local bookstore or use this handy coupon for ordering:

Bantam Books, Inc., Dept. RB, 414 East Golf Road, Des Plaines, Ill. 60016

Please send me the books I have checked above. I am enclosing $_____
(please add $1.25 to cover postage and handling). Send check or money order
—no cash or C.O.D.'s please.

Mr/Mrs/Miss _____

Address_____

City_____State/Zip_____

RB—9/83

Please allow four to six weeks for delivery. This offer expires 3/84.